The Sc
Message of
James

If a brother or sister is naked
and lacks daily food,
and one of you says to them,
"Go in peace; keep warm and eat your fill,"
and yet you do not supply their bodily needs,
what is the good of that?
So faith by itself, if it has no works, is dead.
But someone will say,
"You have faith and I have works."
Show me your faith apart from your works,
and I by my works will show you my faith.
For just as the body without the spirit is dead,
so faith without works is also dead.

—James 2:15–18, 26, NRSV

The Scandalous
Message of
James

Faith Without
Works Is Dead

Revised Edition

Elsa Tamez

STUDY GUIDE BY PAMELA SPARR

A Crossroad Book
The Crossroad Publishing Company
New York

This edition published by
The Crossroad Publishing Company
481 Eighth Avenue, Suite 1550
New York, NY 10001

Scripture quotations are from the Jerusalem Bible © 1966 by Darton, Longman & Todd, Ltd., and Doubleday & Company, Inc.

First presented at the Facultad Metodista de Teología, São Paulo, Brazil, for the Semana Teológica Wesleyana, May 1985.

First published as *Santiago: Lectura latinoamericana de la epístola,* by Editorial DEI, Apartado Postal 390-2070 Sabanilla, San José, Costa Rica.

Printed in the United States of America.

Printed on 60 lb. Pristine Opaque Smooth White chlorine-free 30% recycled paper.

Library of Congress Cataloging-in-Publication Data

Tamez, Elsa.
    [Santiago. English]
    The scandalous message of James : faith without works is dead / Elsa Tamez ; [translated by John Eagleson] ; study guide by Pamela Sparr. – Rev. ed.
        p. cm.
    Includes bibliographical references (p.   ) and indexes.
    ISBN 0-8245-1941-8
    1. Bible. N.T. James – Criticism, interpretation, etc. 2. Christianity and justice – Biblical teaching. 3. Latin America – Church history – 20th century. I. Title.
    BS2785.6.J8 T3513 2002
    227$'$.9106 – dc21

                                        2002000607

1   2   3   4   5   6   7   8   9   10   08   07   06   05   04   03   02

To Lucila and Carlos,
my parents

Contents

Study Guide
The Scandalous Message of James
by Pamela Sparr

Session 3: Exploring the Meaning of Hope
for the Writer of James and Ourselves

Foreword to the Revised Edition

The world-renowned Latin American theologian Dr. Elsa Tamez, who is currently professor of biblical studies at the Latin American Biblical University in Costa Rica, has a prolific record of creative works in theology, particularly in the area of contemporary biblical interpretation. Among them is the first English edition of this book in 1990, which brought to the fore her unique gifts of "exegetical sensitivity and analytical sharpness," as well as her literary talents.

This new volume is again a serious exegetical work: it allows the biblical text to speak for itself, and the original context to take shape through the text. This is done by means of some clarifying devices, such as looking at the text from various angles and perspectives; finding a thread or weaving together passages and concepts; and letting the words shine forth in all their facets in pure Jamesian style: "Listen!" "Behold!"

Many things have changed since 1990. We still live in a world of oppression, growing poverty, warfare, and terrorism — even more so now. The global market, with its contrasting and threatening effects on peoples and life on the planet, is the name of the game. We have entered, indeed sunk, into the postmodern world, a fragmented one in which rationality, the meaning of life, the purpose of human history, and hope in the future are far from clear.

Certainly we live in a world of "trials and temptations" as reflected in the Letter of James (1:2, 12ff.), which was addressed to Christians "in the *Dispersion"[a] during the last

---

a. Words preceded by an asterisk are defined in the Glossary beginning on p. 163.

quarter of the first century. Maybe we are not that far from feeling like "a wave of the sea, driven and tossed by the wind" (1:6), tempted by the "New Age" and other "spiritualities" finally to fall in desperate seeking into the meanders of magic and individualistic mysticism.

So, is there a message — "a word of encouragement and advice" (p. 1) — for us twenty-first-century Christians in the global village from this "open letter" to Christians everywhere? The answer depends on us, the readers and addressees, to receive and read the text with "wisdom from God" (1:5) — if we seek it.

Today, this letter will probably not be intercepted by some authoritarian government, but in our world of misinformation, it might well be dismissed as nonrecyclable material amid the massive cloud of "information" from the media. Still, we can choose to enter into the stimulating and challenging experience of reading and interpreting this biblical text from our own situation with the promise and, yes, the risk of discovery and illumination — even, we may hope, conversion.

Elsa Tamez is an outstanding representative of both Latin American and Mujerista, or feminist, theologies. Little wonder that her many books and articles are in permanent demand from many quarters. Well-deserved was the Hans-Sigrist Prize awarded her in 2000 from the University of Berne, Switzerland, for her outstanding contribution as a biblical scholar, theologian, and university rector.

MORTIMER ARIAS
Bishop Emeritus, Methodist Church

September 2001

– One –

The Intercepted Letter

IF THE LETTER OF JAMES were sent to the Christian communities of certain countries that suffer from violence and exploitation, it would very possibly be intercepted by government security agencies. The document would be branded as subversive because of the paragraphs that vehemently denounce the exploitation by landowners (5:1–6) and the carefree life of the merchants (4:13–17). The passage that affirms that "pure, unspoilt religion, in the eyes of God our Father is this: coming to the help of orphans and widows when they need it, and keeping oneself uncontaminated by the world" (1:27) would be criticized as "*reductionism" of the gospel or as Marxist-Leninist infiltration in the churches. The communities to which the letter was addressed would become very suspicious to the authorities. For postmodern persons of the early twenty-first century, the letter would present an *anachronistic discourse because it does not take into account the complexities of life.

But I am speaking of a very ancient letter written by a man named James to the first Christian churches. We are dealing with a servant of Jesus Christ concerned with the poor and oppressed people of his times, people who were undergoing unbearable suffering and were in need of strength and hope. James offered them a word of encouragement and advice.

Attempts at "Interception" throughout History

Reading the history of this document (similar to that of other documents, although this has been more consistently dispar-

aged than many), we realize that there is something in the
letter that has made church authorities regard it with suspicion. Although the letter was probably written at the end
of the first century or the beginning of the second, it was
not finally accepted as part of the *canon until the end of
the fourth century, and in some churches it continued to be
questioned in subsequent centuries.[1]

Challenges to the letter did not end after the formation of
the canon. At the beginning of the sixteenth century (1516)
*Erasmus, in his *Annotationes* to the first printed edition of
the Greek New Testament, again mentions the problems surrounding the canonical recognition of the letter. Referring to
the language and style of the letter, he added his own doubts
regarding its *apostolic authorship.

A few years after Erasmus, the letter suffered the most fe-
rocious attacks at the hands of Martin *Luther. Who doesn't
recall the famous phrase "the epistle of straw" on hearing
the name of James? Unfortunately, at the popular level the
best-known commentaries on James are those of Luther.

Luther could not accept the Letter of James, nor could he
accept Hebrews, Jude, or Revelation. But it was the Letter
of James that he most disdained. For him the letter was not
faithful to the gospel of Christ, namely, according to Luther,
the doctrine of salvation by faith. In his preface to the first
edition of the New Testament, he asserts:

> St. John's Gospel and his first epistle, St. Paul's epis-
> tles, especially Romans, Galatians, and Ephesians, and
> St. Peter's first epistle are the books that show you
> Christ and teach you all that is necessary and salvatory
> for you to know, even if you were never to see or hear
> any other book or doctrine. Therefore St. James' epistle
> is really an epistle of straw, compared to these others,
> for it has nothing of the nature of the gospel about it.[2]

Luther placed the books of James, Hebrews, Jude, and
Revelation at the end of his German translation of the New
Testament, but he assigned them no numbers in his table

of contents. The modern edition of Luther's translation of the German Bible still puts these books at the end of the New Testament—but they are included in the table of contents. The disdain for the letter continued. So, for example, according to Donald Guthrie, nineteenth-century *biblical criticism considered the letter to be a product of a brand of Christianity inferior to Pauline theology.[3]

We wonder why there were so many "buts" involved before the letter was recognized as a part of the gospel message. The reasons are various and of very different nature. Apostolic authorship was one of the most important criteria used by the early church to determine a document's inclusion in the canon. The letters of Paul and the Gospels were quickly included. Because of uncertain authorship, others took longer. The Letter of James was a candidate from the beginning, but it was often questioned whether the author was James the brother of the Lord.

Why did the letter come to be known so late? Some believe that originally the letter did not carry the name of James, and so it was considered unimportant; but there is no basis for such an affirmation. Martin Dibelius, the well-known biblical scholar, believed that the lack of mention has to do with the *paraenetic character of the letter. He says that a document of moral exhortations is relevant at a certain time and for certain circumstances, and later such exhortations became obsolete. But when James was recognized as the brother of the Lord, the document was reevaluated.[4]

As we read the central message of James, though, we wonder when a document that defends the oppressed from injustice becomes irrelevant. For there have always been oppressed people.

Another of the objections to the letter is that there is little mention of Jesus, or little *Christology. But is it not James who makes most mention of the sayings of Jesus? The Sermon on the Mount appears almost in its entirety in the letter.[5] Why should we give importance to what is said about Jesus and not to what Jesus said?

In Luther's case it is clear that the Letter of James did not fit into his doctrine of justification by faith alone. Using the very words of Paul, although with a different meaning as we shall see, James asserts that faith without works is dead and that a person is justified by works and not only by faith (2:24). We should not level anachronistic criticisms at Luther, nor assert that he totally rejected the letter. Luther recognizes that it was written by a pious man (according to him, the son of Zebedee). He accepts its position on the law of God, but he does not give it *apostolic authority. As he says: "I will not have it in my Bible in the number of the proper chief books but do not intend thereby to forbid anyone to place and exalt it as he pleases, for there is many a good saying in it."[6] Nevertheless, we have to recognize that his comments have been in large part responsible for the secondary position of the letter today.

This is a letter that is important for us to recover and reread today. Notwithstanding all its difficulties, the letter was not "intercepted." It has survived, thanks to its defenders throughout Christian history and to the Holy Spirit. Today nobody doubts its authenticity as part of our canon.

Still, although it might seem strange, we can say that the attempts at unconscious "interception" still continue. For example:

a. There is a surprising dearth of literature on the letter in Spanish and in other languages. This is probably due to the privileged place given to abstract thought in our Western societies. The reasonableness of faith is valued more than the practice of faith; the latter is seen as separate from the former, or as a product of faith's reasonableness. That is, ethics, behavior, deeds are considered of secondary importance by our *logocentric societies. Thus a letter like that of James, which focuses its attention on the daily practice of Christian life, is easily *marginalized, while the "theological" letters of Paul are highly esteemed. It is not unusual, moreover, that in many churches, at least the Protestant churches, Paul is read and quoted more than the Gospels, which speak of the life of

Jesus. In other words, the letter is not attractive, in the eyes of the wise.

    b. James's radical critique of the rich has contributed to this "crafty theft" of the letter. I know of churches where the letter is skipped over in the liturgies because there are many rich members in the congregation, and it is very uncomfortable to speak against them when they are sitting in the front seats. Certain parts of James, especially chapter 5, are very concrete and thus very difficult to "spiritualize."

    c. Certain experts have also contributed to the "interception." Dibelius, for example, compartmentalizes the letter when he asserts its paraenetic character, that is, he says that it is a series of moral exhortations presented with certain characteristics. He takes this literary style as his point of departure and then asserts that the sayings have no connection among themselves and that any *exegesis that attempts to unite them is artificial.[7] In this way Dibelius ties the hands of the reader or *exegete who attempts to do a rereading of the letter.

    Peter Davids, professor of biblical studies at Trinity Episcopal School for Ministry, says that we must go beyond Dibelius's *form criticism to discover the *redactional level of the Letter of James.[8] I would add that we must place ourselves at a certain distance from Dibelius in this regard to provide a reading meaningful for our situation today. Every saying or tradition that James uses has its own history, as Dibelius well demonstrates. But these sayings as used by James in relation to others clearly take on a new meaning, for they now form part of another text in another context.

    Peter Davids handles the letter more freely and even tries to give it a structure and situate it historically. But in the end his assertions have little attraction for those involved with liberation concerns, for he says that it is not up to Christians to take the judgment of the rich oppressors into their own hands, but rather that God will do that at the end of time.[9]

    These are just two examples among many others.

d. We must recognize that for those of us who want to read the text from the perspective of the poor, it will be difficult for us to accept passages like James 1:2, which says, "My brothers, you will always have your trials but, when they come, try to treat them as a happy privilege." We may very well decide to read a different biblical text with a more obvious meaning for liberation. By doing this we too contribute to "intercepting" the Letter of James, which we so much need to recover today in Latin America.

General Characteristics of the Letter

With regard to the date, the authorship, and the geographical origin of the letter, there is no consensus among the experts. For instance, two commentaries differ markedly. Sophie Laws (1980), professor in New Testament at King's College, University of London, asserts that the author is someone who took the name of James as a *pseudonym, a common practice in Jewish and Greco-Roman literature.[10] Laws situates the letter in Rome due to its similarity to other literature like 1 Peter, Clement of Rome, and *Hermas.[11] Laws dates the letter between 70 and 130 C.E.

Peter Davids (1982) believes that the author was James, the brother of the Lord, and that perhaps later someone else edited the letter.[12] For Davids, the letter has its origin in Palestine. He attempts to establish its *Sitz im Leben,* which many others do not attempt. He bases his argument on the mention of farmers and merchants in the letter. He analyzes the groups that existed in Palestine before the fall of Jerusalem (45–65) and after (75–85) to help determine the period during which the letter was edited.[13]

Others with the name of James have been proposed as the author: James, the son of *Alpheus, and James, the son of Zebedee. These are no longer accepted by the majority of scholars.

Egypt and Syria have been suggested as the place of origin of the letter. So, depending on the author and its origin, the dates for the letter range between 40 and 130; quite a span, indeed.

The matter is quite complex and has been long debated, for the letter has very special characteristics that lend credence to a number of theories. To insist that these characteristics are a reflection of its paraenetic character does not resolve the problem.

What we can say with certainty is that the author was Jewish;[14] he knows the Hebrew Scriptures thoroughly, and, keeping in mind the *rabbinic tradition, we note *Semitic expressions in his Greek. He was a Christian; he uses many of the sayings of Jesus and speaks of the practices of the early church (5:13–18). And finally, the author betrays significant *Hellenic influence, which is seen not only in some of his commentaries, but also and especially in his manner of writing Greek as his mother tongue. According to some, the best Greek in the New Testament is found in the letter; James uses sixty-three words (*hapax legomena*) that appear nowhere else in the New Testament.[15]

Because of the controversial nature of the letter and the uncertainty with regard to author, date, and place of origin, we will leave this debate and turn to the text itself, in the light of our own context. For us the author is a man named James, who calls himself a servant of Jesus Christ. He could embody all the Jameses we know, the son of the carpenter, brother of the Lord, and great leader of the church of Jerusalem. He could also be the son of the fisherman, or a teacher (3:1), or any other. He is a person concerned about the well-being of the oppressed Christian communities and about the poor in general. What matters is not so much the true identity of this man, but rather his message for us today. When did he write the letter? At a time when there was suffering and oppression. Where did he write it? Any place in the world where the Christian communities needed it. This is one of the so-called universal, or catholic, epistles.

A Proposal for a Latin American Reading of the Letter

We are going to try to recover for our people this letter abandoned and disdained by so many. It is not easy to penetrate it. Its style is very different from letters we read today. A first reading leaves us disconcerted. When we finish, many themes come to mind, apparently unconnected, some repeated. Because of its style, it is difficult to grasp the structure of the letter (paraenetic, with frequent *diatribe).[16] The scholars do not agree about the structure. Many simply analyze the different themes separately, or chapter by chapter.[17] We choose to perceive a framework, a scene, a picture.

The first reading of the letter is like the first approach of a photographer to the subject: much is perceived and little is perceived; there is no clarity; the image is out of focus. So at the end of our first reading we can make a long list of themes and important terms, but we're not sure what we're dealing with, what is the principal theme, and other like matters that we easily recognize when we read other writings of the New Testament. Following the order of the letter, the list will be more or less the following:

Chapter 1

greetings
joy, testing, tested faith
patience, suffering, *perfect works, integrity
prayer, wisdom
vacillation, lack of constancy
the exalted poor, the humiliated rich
happiness, resistance, testing, crown of life
God does not tempt, *concupiscence, sin, death
good gift from on high
God—Word of truth—life
quick to listen, slow to speak, slow to anger
anger does not serve the justice of God
undo the evil and accept the planted word

do the word, not only hear it
perfect law of freedom
tongue, control, deception
vain religion, pure religion (to visit the orphans and
    widows and keep oneself uncontaminated by the
    world)

Chapter 2

no favoritism
rich-poor, God chooses the poor
the rich oppress, they drag the poor before tribunals
    and blaspheme the name (of the Lord)
the royal law according to the Scriptures (to love our
    neighbor as ourselves)
speak and work according to the law of liberty
judgment, mercy
faith and works together
justification by works and not by faith alone
faith without works is dead

Chapter 3

do not make yourselves teachers, judgment
to sin by speaking, the tongue (examples)
wisdom, good conduct
false wisdom, true wisdom
the fruits of justice are sown in peace for those who
    assure peace

Chapter 4

war, contentiousness, greed, wastefulness
prayer
friendship with God
submit to God, resist the devil
purify yourself
do not speak evil of others
judgment
the arrogance of the merchants, sin

Chapter 5

weep, you rich; rotten wealth
accumulation of wealth, salaries of the workers who
     cry out
God hears the cries of the laborers
the just do not resist
patience, the coming of the Lord (example)
do not lose heart
do not complain about each other
suffering (of the prophets), Job
blessing, patience, compassionate and merciful
     Lord
no swearing (simply say yes or no)
prayer (examples)
confess to each other, the power of fervent prayer
convert the one who strays from the truth

We might note that many of the ideas are to be found in
the first chapter. Nearly the entire content of the letter appears there, so it strikes us as quite dense, difficult, and even
incoherent. It is presented in units that seem to be disconnected. It would seem that the only link between the units
is the catchword, the final word of one saying that is repeated in the following, for example, *chairein* with *charan*
(to greet–joy), *leipomenoi* with *leipetai* (lacking–lack).

In chapters 2 through 4 we see an elaboration of the
themes announced in the first chapter and one or another
new theme (for example, the call to conversion in 4:7–10).
At the end of the letter we note that the main themes of
the first chapter are taken up again: judgment against the
rich, patience, prayer, suffering, consistency between words
and deeds.

The framework is still not clear. We must focus more
sharply, that is, read the letter again, several times. When
we see the letter more clearly, we can look at it from three
angles, each distinct but complementary.

The Angle of Oppression-Suffering

There is a community of believers (*adelphoi mou*) that suffers. There is a group of rich people who oppress them and drag them before the tribunals. There are peasants who are exploited, Christian and non-Christian, by the rich farmers who accumulate wealth at the expense of the workers' salaries. There is a class of merchants who lead a carefree life, with no concern for the poor.

The Angle of Hope

This community of believers needs a word of hope, of encouragement, of reassurance concerning the end of the injustice. James gives it to them from the very beginning of his letter. We see hope in his greeting, his insistence on declaring the community happy, *makarios,* in his words about God's preference for the poor, God's judgment against the oppressors, the anticipated end of the oppression, and the coming of the Lord.

The Angle of *Praxis

The content of the letter is concentrated in this angle. For James the denunciation of the present situation and the announcement of hope are not sufficient. Something more is needed: praxis. He asks of these Christians a praxis in which they show a militant patience, a consistency between words, belief, and deeds, a prayer with power, an effective wisdom and an unconditional, sincere love among the members of the community.

This is the picture that I see with the eyes of an "oppressed and believing" people. This is the focus I will give to the letter.

– *Two* –

The Angle of Oppression

JAMES PRESENTS US with a picture that can be viewed from different angles. One of these is the situation of oppression experienced by James's listeners and other persons who were part of the picture. Some scholars who concentrate solely on the analysis of form criticism point out that James simply brings together the *Hebrew Bible and rabbinic tradition through sayings, proverbs, admonitions, etc.[1] They say that these are disconnected and do not necessarily have anything to do with current issues, such as, for example, favoritism or judgment against the rich.

It is true that some of the sayings are used as they appear in the Hebrew Bible, especially in the Greek version, or *Septuagint, and that the ferocity with which James attacks the rich is very similar to the tone of the Psalms and the prophets. Nonetheless, this in no way means that James did not take his inspiration from the present to take the tradition, select from it, and reread it in his own context. Sophie Laws asserts, "It seems reasonable, then, to suppose that the inclusion of a teaching on rich and poor, thus creatively presented, reflects a real concern of the author himself."[2] Along the same lines, Peter Davids notes that we cannot find in the letter a clear and specific historical situation, nor a clearly defined crisis like that of 1 Corinthians or 1 Thessalonians. Nonetheless, he says, "it is hard to understand how the choice of this material could not reflect the *Sitz im Leben* of the author, his readers, or both."[3]

For us there is no doubt that oppression is one of the principal motives that compelled the author to write the letter.

He made use of other materials both ancient and contemporary, phrases, sayings, familiar proverbs, but he gave them a new meaning related to his day. Each of these materials has its own history, as Dibelius has excellently analyzed. But I believe that each such unit, as it becomes part of another text and is articulated with other units, offers a new and relevant meaning. When we write a letter or a meditation, we can include passages of poetry or well-known phrases. But we give to those passages the meaning that we wish, or we understand them in the light of our own context, and that is how they will be understood by our readers. Preformed units, employed in another text, tell us more about the present situation of the new text than they do about the times in which they originated,[4] although they do of course maintain a close relationship with the original meaning. Thus we have before us a new and relevant letter that reflects a situation of injustice and oppression and that challenges Christians to confront that situation.

There are certain details in the picture that help us perceive the angle of oppression. One of them is the author's insistence on recommending patience to his listeners (1:3, 5:7). This is a signal that his readers or the communities that he has in mind are undergoing difficult problems. There are other similar indicators, for example:

the twelve tribes in the Dispersion;
being surrounded by all kinds of trials;
patience in suffering;
the brother in a lowly condition should glory in his
    exaltation, and the rich in his humiliation;
happy are those who endure the trial;
widows and orphans in oppression;
the rich oppress and drag the poor before the tribunals;
someone lacks food and clothing (2:15);
envy and the spirit of contentiousness, arrogance, lies;
war as the result of passions, pride;
we will bargain and we will gain;

the one who knows how to do good and does not do it
    commits sin;
the accumulation of wealth;
unpaid workers;
the cries of the workers are reaching the ears of
    the Lord;
condemnation and death of the just one, who does not
    resist;
have patience, strengthen your hearts because the
    coming of the Lord is near;
suffering and patience of the prophets, etc.

All these phrases interspersed throughout the letter give
us hints of the problem that the communities faced. We do
not know with certainty if these communities were in Rome,
Egypt, Palestine, or another part of Asia Minor. But we can
be sure about the experience of oppression that pervades the
letter.

On the basis of the phrases in the letter we can de-
duce that there were two antagonistic groups: the poor and
the rich, the oppressed and the oppressors. There are conflicts within the group of the oppressed. At certain points in
the letter the line between oppressors and oppressed is not
clear, but the implicit conflicts can be perceived. There are
both Christians and non-Christians among the oppressed.
And there are both Christians and non-Christians among
the oppressors, especially the rich. We can also observe
the experience of oppression and the mechanisms that the
oppressors use.

The Oppressed

The oppressed in the Epistle of James are principally the
poor. Various studies have already been published relating
poverty with oppression. The poor are poor generally because they are oppressed and exploited; the oppressed are
the impoverished. In the Hebrew Bible there are various

Hebrew words that denote oppression, and there are also various words to designate the poor (*daka'*, *'anah*, *'asaq*, *rasas*, *nagas*, *lajas*, *yanah*, *takak*, and others). Very often the word "poor" and the verb "to oppress" appear together, thus showing the close relationship between poverty and oppression. It is not uncommon, moreover, to find the word "robbery" between both terms, as well as the word "violence."[5] "The people of the country have taken to extortion [*'asaq*] and banditry; they have oppressed [*yanah*] the poor and needy and have ill-treated the settler for no reason" (Ezek. 22:29).

In James the relationship is clear among poverty, oppression, exploitation, and violence. Chapter 5 first calls our attention to the scene we have been considering. James says, "Laborers mowed your fields, and you cheated them — listen to the wages that you kept back, calling out; realize that the cries of the reapers have reached the ears of the Lord of hosts" (5:4). The author uses the Semitic expression "listen," "behold," to call attention to the great injustice that is being committed. Oppression, as well as holding back salaries, was explicitly prohibited in the Hebrew Bible: "You must not exploit or rob your neighbor. You must not keep back the laborer's wage until next morning" (Lev. 19:13).

The *Deuteronomist also refers to this law:

> You are not to exploit the hired servant who is poor and destitute, whether he is one of your brothers or a stranger who lives in your towns. You must pay him his wage each day, not allowing the sun to set before you do, for he is poor and is anxious for it; otherwise he may appeal to Yahweh against you, and it would be a sin for you. (Deut. 24:14)

The prophets continuously denounce the oppression of the workers. Note, for example, the famous passage from the prophet Jeremiah:

> Doom for the man who founds his palace on anything
>   but integrity,
> his upstairs rooms on anything but honesty,
> who makes his fellow man work for nothing,
> without paying him his wages. (22:13)

There are many other texts like these. James rereads this tradition in the light of his own context. The peasants (*ergatēs*) also live in wretchedness because of the oppressors. The landowners could very well pay the salaries, but they hold them back. Various texts read *apesterēmenos,* which means "to rob"; others say *aphysterēmenos,* "to withhold,"[6] not in the sense of delaying, but rather of not paying at all.[7] Either text results in the same conclusion: the workers are without their salaries.

To withhold the salaries of the workers is to attack their very lives. In many cases slaves had more protection than the laborers, because the slaves could at least depend on food and shelter from their owners. The laborers, on the other hand, depended completely on their salaries. In the times of Jesus, according to Joachim Jeremias, a German biblical scholar, there were more day laborers than slaves. Day laborers earned on the average a denarius, that is to say, the minimum needed for one day's survival including their meal. This salary was already low, but for day laborers it was very serious not to find work or not to be paid.[8] For this reason James personifies the salary, seeing it as the very blood of the exploited workers crying out pitifully. The case was the same for the peasants. The peasants die because they pour out their strength in their work, but the fruit of their work does not come back to them. They cannot regain their strength because the rich withhold their salaries. Therefore James accuses the rich of condemning and killing the just (5:6).

The cries of the just are incoherent. In Greek literature the term *boē,* "cry," is used for the howls of wild animals.[9] In the Septuagint (LXX) it appears frequently as a protest against injustice. Recall the blood of Abel that cried out for vengeance for murder. In Exodus 2:23 the Hebrew slaves in Egypt cried out in their oppression with these same cries. The peasants, then, cry out in a heart-rending way as a sign of protest, of denunciation of the injustice. It is a cry that beseeches the Lord for vengeance.[10]

The Letter of James does not tell us if these oppressed people were Christians or not. More important for him is the experience of death suffered by the poor, who are creatures of God. And it is made very clear in the letter that God, the giver of life, hears them. We can conclude that among these poor were members of the communities that James was addressing, and that this exploitation was one of the principal reasons for their suffering. James 5:7 provides substantiation for this conclusion.

Another group of oppressed people mentioned in the letter are the widows and orphans (1:27). In the Hebrew Bible these groups continually appear as representatives of the oppressed classes. They are poor and oppressed because they have no one to defend them, nor can they defend themselves. They are truly helpless. Everyone takes advantage of them, especially those in power, such as the judges, the political leaders, and the priests. In the tradition of the Hebrew Bible they are the object of the love of God and those who seek to do the will of God.[11]

Jesus is also attentive to the widows; he marveled at a poor widow who gave her two last coins (Mark 12:41–44), and he criticized the scribes who often exploited the widows (Mark 12:40). In the early church, the orphans and widows were also a major concern.[12] Interest in this class of oppressed poor was such that James defines true religion as visiting and helping them, that is, spending time with them, joining them in their oppression, and sharing basic necessities with them.[13]

The word used for oppression in this text is the Greek term *thlipsis,* commonly translated as "tribulation," "difficulty," "affliction," etc. Thomas Hanks, a biblical scholar and a missionary in Latin America, analyzes the term as used here and in different parts of the New Testament, and he criticizes the ambiguity of the translations that hide the true and scandalous meaning of oppression and economic exploitation.[14] As for the Letter of James, Hanks asserts that his study leads to the conclusion that the translations hide in a systematic way many of the texts of the New Testament that do indeed speak of oppression.[15]

A manuscript of the seventeenth century reads in 1:27, " ... protect them [referring to the needy: widows and orphans] from the world," instead of "keeping oneself uncontaminated by the world." The world as it is structured is hostile to the poor, for it keeps them out of the system constructed by the rulers and the powerful for their own benefit. James, then, urges that they be protected from the oppressive world. This *variant makes more sense in this passage.[16]

Another group of oppressed people that appears in the letter are those to whom the letter is addressed. Up until now James has spoken of the oppressed in general: peasants, widows, and orphans, many of whom, of course, belonged to Christian communities. Thus the radical judgment against the rich and the constant call to patience. But let us look now at the communities of "the brothers and sisters" to whom the letter is addressed.

The title of the addressees is noteworthy: "the twelve tribes in the Dispersion." The phrase is much debated; only 1 Peter and James use the word "dispersion" in a greeting to Christians. Some hold that James uses the term as a symbol of the new and true Israel to address converted Jews or non-Jewish converts to Christianity who live outside Palestine. John H. Elliott, professor of theology and religious studies at the University of San Francisco, in an interesting sociological analysis of 1 Peter, holds that this term indicates religious identity as well as a displaced and alien social condition.[17] Elliott analyzes *paroikia, paroikos, parepidēmos,* and **diaspora* as related terms connoting a community of Christians marginalized by and in tension with their social neighbors because of their Christian faith.

The word *diaspora* does not refer exclusively to Jews or gentiles. The meaning of the term is figurative and implies transitoriness; it is a sociological expression and characterizes the position of Christians in Greco-Roman society. These were displaced persons who were currently aliens or were permanently or temporarily residing in Asia Minor. They suffered political, legal, social, and religious restrictions.

Elliott believes that the word *diaspora* in James 1:1 has the same connotation as in 1 Peter. The author of the epistle, then, employs the figure of the twelve tribes, nomadic clans, who were homeless and lived as displaced foreigners both in Egypt and Babylon. The Christians of the Letter of James, like the people of ancient Israel, experienced that same religious and social *marginalization. Today many rely on 1 Peter to develop the idea that we live as pilgrims in this world, awaiting the next. Elliott criticizes this position that evades reality, asserting that to be a pilgrim or to live in the *diaspora* is a sociological designation of the Christian movement and not a *cosmological theology.

If we accept Elliott's proposal regarding the meaning of *diaspora*, we find in the Letter of James a community or communities of Christians, or brothers (*adelphoi*), marginalized or deprived of the civil, social, and political rights of the cities or regions in which they lived.

Within this community of marginalized people we observe different social strata: the poor, the less poor, and those who live more comfortably.

The poor were the *ptōchoi*,[18] a Greek term designating those who totally lacked the means of subsistence and lived from alms; they were the beggars. The poor were also the *penēs*,[19] those who at least had a job but owned no property. Both groups were exploited by the rich and powerful, and thus the terms often function as synonyms. Curiously, the New Testament speaks more of *ptōchos*. According to Wolfgang Stegemann, professor of New Testament at the Augustana

Hochschule in Germany, the number of these increased greatly during the period of the Roman Empire; therefore, he says, "the predominant use of *ptōchos* in the New Testament must be understood also as a reflection of a social reality."[20] In James we have these poor, *ptōchoi,* present within the community,[21] for example, in 2:15: "If one of the brothers or one of the sisters is in need of clothes and has not enough food to live on...." A poor person, *ptōchos,* also appears as a visitor to the church (2:2). The widows and orphans (1:27) must be counted among the poor. Jesus calls a widow *ptōchos* (Mark 12:43). The peasant of chapter 5 would not be a poor person in the sense of *ptōchos* but rather of *penēs,* because he has a job. Nonetheless, as we have seen, many of them became *ptōchos* when they were not paid.

In James 2:6 the author clearly recognizes that the members of the communities were oppressed by the rich and taken off by force to the courts. Nevertheless, they too, or at least some of them, tended to discriminate against the poor, *ptōchoi,* either because they didn't suffer the level of extreme poverty of the *ptōchoi* or because, despite being in the same position as the *ptōchoi,* they tended to favor the rich. James calls their attention to this favoritism and reminds them that the poor are precisely the ones who shall inherit the reign promised to those who love God (2:5).

Reading the letter from a woman's viewpoint, we are sensitive to the double oppression of women, because of both their class and their sex. It is noteworthy that James specifies the feminine sex in 2:15: "If one of the brothers [*adelphos*] or one of the sisters [*adelphē*]...," for the word "brother" was frequently used both in the singular and the plural to designate both sexes. It is very probable, then, that the needy were commonly women. Otherwise, given the *patriarchal environment of the origin of the letter, the word *adelphos* would have been sufficient. Moreover, the patriarchal language is confirmed in James's use in several places of the word *anēr* ("man," "male") instead of *anthrōpos* ("human being") to refer to both sexes. In 1:12, for example, he says,

"Happy the man. . . . " *Anēr* corresponds strictly to the word "male," just as *gynē* corresponds to "female." *Anthrōpos* would be the most appropriate word in this verse, as a generic term. Due to the *androcentric environment, however, the use of the word *anēr* as a synonym of *anthrōpos* was not unusual.[22]

The Oppressors: Characteristics and Mechanisms

For James the oppressors are the rich (*plousioi*). He does not hesitate to point them out as such. His antipathy toward them and his sympathy with the poor is undeniable. Interestingly enough, many of the commentaries on James dedicate long pages to the rich, thus consciously or unconsciously attempting to relativize this contrasting picture that James paints. It is said that he is simply relying on a familiar ancient tradition, or that he is employing an *apocalyptic or paraenetic style, or that the rich are bad non-Christian Jews, or that he is giving very general examples that have no concrete historical reference point, or that the poor are the pious Christians while the rich are not.

This great concentration on the rich is to be expected: on the one hand, many biblical commentaries from Europe and the United States are written in situations where there are many rich people in the churches. How does one tell these members that according to James there is no room for them in the church? We should note that many of the points made in these commentaries are accurate enough; what is striking is simply the angle of the perspective and the special concern for the rich. A Latin American reading of the epistle, on the other hand, fixes its gaze on the oppressed and dedicates long pages to them, their sufferings, complaints, oppression, hope, and praxis. From the angle of oppression with which we are reading James, we must adopt the perspective of the oppressed, which, we believe, is that of James. And so we have *first* identified the *oppressed,* and all our subsequent comments will be offered from that perspective.

The rich oppressors are referred to three times and in a totally negative manner. We see them first in 1:10–11 in a sarcastic phrase: "It is right for...the rich one to be thankful that he has been humbled, because riches last no longer than the flowers in the grass...." Later in 2:6b, 7, we read, "Isn't it always the rich who are against you? Isn't it always their doing when you are dragged before the court? Aren't they the ones who insult the honorable name to which you have been dedicated?" Finally, in 5:5–6 James says: "On earth you have had a life of comfort and luxury; in the time of slaughter you went on eating to your heart's content. It was you who condemned the innocent and killed them; they offered you no resistance."

The first appearance and the third occur within a judgment. In the second the author describes the customary behavior of those of the oppressing class.

The fierce attack against the rich suggests acute problems between the social classes. James's appropriation of the prophetic tradition of Amos, Isaiah, Jeremiah, Micah, and others is not fortuitous. His concern for the poor and oppressed, like that of Jesus, arises from his real-life situation. In his study *Property and Riches in the Early Church*, Martin Hengel, professor at the University of Tübingen in Germany, describes how the exploitation by the landowners intensified during the Hellenistic period, after Alexander, and how the Romans and their rulers (Herod and his successors) exploited the land, leaving the peasants without any.[23]

At the time of Jesus, social divisions were acute both in Palestine and throughout the Roman Empire. Joachim Jeremias describes the families of the high priests, rich and powerful, who exploited the pilgrims who came to the temple and other members of the rural clergy.[24] When we read about this deplorable situation we can understand why Jesus was so hard on the powerful groups.

James follows the line of Jesus' prophetic preaching. He does not speak of the poor in the pietistic sense common in later Judaism; nor does he follow the rabbinic tradition of retribution, which affirmed that riches were the blessing of God.[25] For James poverty is the result of a scandalous act of oppression.

The rich, as James describes them, have the following characteristics:

a. Unlike the poor, they dress elegantly (2:2). "Now suppose a man comes into your synagogue, beautifully dressed and with a gold ring on, and at the same time a poor man comes in, in shabby clothes...."

According to Sophie Laws, the gold ring may signify more than just ordinary wealth. It also suggests official social status, "for the gold ring was part of the insignia of the equestrian order, the second level of the Roman aristocracy."[26] The expression "beautifully dressed" seems to have been the customary term to indicate very expensive clothing.[27] This depiction of the rich man refers to his power and wealth, whether or not he is a Roman official.

b. The rich are those who oppress the poor and drag them before the courts (2:6). James uses the Greek word *katadynasteuō* for oppression. This word is frequently used in the Septuagint and signifies oppression, exploitation by the abuse of power.[28] The subjects of these verbs are the rich and powerful, and the objects are the poor and weak.[29] In this case the oppressed are those of the Christian community, made up primarily of the poor. The rich oblige the poor to appear in court to extract taxes from them and legally to force them to pay their debts.

c. Not only are the rich estranged from those who have nothing, they are anxious to acquire more and scheme to get it (4:13). "Here is the answer for those of you who talk like this: 'Today or tomorrow, we are off to this or that town; we are going to spend a year there, trading, and make some money.'"

James criticizes these rich (although he doesn't use the term), and those who would be rich, because they think of themselves as if they were isolated individuals with no relationship to the wretchedness around them. James tells them that before they make their plans they should say, "If it is the Lord's will, we shall still be alive to do this or that" (4:15). And this should not be merely a slogan or a prayer for God's blessing on their enterprise; rather they should consider what God's will really is, whether God approves of their activities and wants them to live only for themselves. James accuses them of committing sin because they know how to do good and do not do it.

d. They accumulate wealth (5:3). This is the principal characteristic and motivation of oppression, as frequently described in the Hebrew Bible.[30] Jesus is also against hoarding, for this is always done at the expense of the oppressed. In such wealth is found the wages of the peasants.

e. They live luxuriously, devoted to their pleasures (5:5). "On earth you have had a life of comfort and luxury; in the time of slaughter you went on eating to your heart's content." While the rich of 4:13 plan to work and trade to earn their wealth in a selfish way, these rich indulge in the easy life, making others work for them to maintain their luxuries and pleasures.

f. They condemn and kill the just person (5:6). "It was you who condemned the innocent and killed them; they offered you no resistance." The oppressors are murderers, for they condemn to death the just person, the innocent person, the one who has done no wrong, the poor person who has no strength to resist.

These are the characteristics of the rich, familiar to the prophets and to Jesus. It is no wonder James has been called the Amos of the New Covenant.[31]

Rich Persons in the Christian Community?

We still need to discuss a final question important for many of our churches today: Were the rich oppressors Christians? Did they belong to James's community? For the poor today the question is perhaps not so important, for what they care about is that their oppression be recognized and that

Jesus and James identify with them and reject their oppression. Still we must recognize that for many of our Protestant churches this is a concern.

It seems that at the beginning the churches were made up largely of poor people. Celsus, a philosopher of the second century known for his attacks on Christianity, refers to Christians disdainfully, alleging that the church deliberately excluded educated people since the religion was attractive only to the foolish, dishonorable, and stupid, and only slaves, women, and little children (*Contra Celsum*, 111:53). Nevertheless, some scholars have concluded that different social strata emerged within the churches.[32] In the Epistle of James the church is still made up mostly of the poor. Thomas Hanks calls it the brotherhood of the poor.[33] Other social strata, however, can be discerned. There are poor who have nothing, not even a job; they live from alms (2:15). There are others who can earn a living and have a job, but they are poor and very much exploited (5:1–6). Still others tend to look down on those who are poorer (2:6); they could be less poor or just as poor but with a value system that favors the rich. Finally it seems that there are some in the community who enjoy a more comfortable economic position, who are almost rich (4:13–17). Curiously enough, James does not call this group brothers nor does he call them rich; he simply calls them "you who talk..." (*oi legontes*). I believe that they are members of the Christian community since James reproaches them for not consulting the Lord about their plans and for not sharing what they earn with the poor.

The rich (*plousioi*) in the letter do not belong to the Christian community, or at least the author does not think they should belong to it. Of the three contexts in which they are explicitly named, in two they are clearly oppressors (2:6, 5:1–6), and in the third they are condemned to failure in all their pursuits (1:11). It is clear that this judgment is because they oppress others. It seems, then, that at this level of the early church, which began as a poor church, the Christian community began to open widely to the rich, a development that James did not look upon with favor. For him, the poor are "the more natural potential members of the community of faith."[34] In any case, faced with this growing and inevitable incorporation of high social strata,[35] James insists that the vocation of the church, its mission, is the poor, who are rich in faith and the heirs of God's reign (2:5).

– *Three* –

The Angle of Hope

We have looked at the letter from the angle of oppression. Now we will change our perspective and look at it from the angle of hope.

If we compare our reading of the text of James with the experience of being in a dark room, we will immediately realize that it is full of "cracks of hope," reasons for rejoicing. For the entire Bible, in the last analysis, is a proposal for rejoicing. This is not any "vain, *ephemeral joy," but rather a joy whose source is the proclamation of the end of oppression, the end of the corruption of human beings, who are the agents of oppression; in other words, it is the proclamation of the end of sin. The poor and oppressed rejoice because they hear the good news of a promise of liberation. Hope is the core of that experience; we hope with confidence in the promise of liberation and rejoice in anticipation. This is to have faith; this is truly to believe.

The author of the Letter of James is eager to impart this note of hope to his readers. Oppression, suffering, persecution, and experiences mentioned in the letter are not the end of human beings, nor of the Christian communities to whom James writes. He knows this very well, and therefore he emphasizes the need for hope. For only with hope are we moved to action. Hope not only keeps us afloat in oppressive situations, but it strengthens us to overcome these situations.

The details that help us to perceive the hope dimension are various: the greeting, the insistence on declaring "happy the one who...," the phrase "consider supremely happy the one who...." Moreover, he speaks of the poor as the chosen ones, the heirs of the reign of God. He proclaims to those in a lowly condition that they are already able to rejoice in their future exaltation. He cites the Septuagint passage Proverbs 3:34: "God resists the proud and gives grace to the humble" (see in the Hebrew Bible Isa. 2:11, 17; Job 22:29). And, above all, he proclaims judgment against the rich and for the oppressed and the coming of the Lord as the end of oppression. All these details suggest that one of the basic purposes of the author is to inspire hope in the suffering Christian communities and perhaps in the poor who are not members of those communities but happen to read or know of this letter. Let us look more closely at these "cracks of hope."

The Greeting

It is worth taking a closer look at the greeting for two reasons: first, the double identification of the author, on the one hand with God and Jesus Christ, and on the other with those in the Dispersion; second, the use of the Greek infinitive *chairein* for the greeting, which means literally "to have joy" or, here, "may joy be with you."[1]

The author introduces himself in a very simple way: he calls himself a servant, a slave of God and Jesus Christ. He is one who worships God and shows it by doing God's will, that is, by serving. He does not introduce himself as a great leader of the church, nor does he claim to be a relative of Jesus (if in fact the author is James "the just," the brother of the Lord). Nor does he present himself as a teacher, which he apparently was, according to 3:1. Nor does he even refer to himself as an apostle, a prestigious title that Paul uses in Galatians. Rather he introduces himself very humbly: "James, servant of God and of the Lord Jesus Christ."

He addresses people who are oppressed, who suffer, as we have seen. Those of the Dispersion are the Christian communities who are outcast and despised in the societies where they live. The majority are poor or very poor. So the author approaches them and attempts to identify with them, to be as they are, to be in solidarity with them. This is just as God has always done and so too God's son Jesus Christ. Curiously James refers to both—God and Jesus Christ—thus showing continuity between the Hebrew Bible and the New Testament. Such an identification with those who suffer is in itself a reason for joy.

The author uses the term *chairein* for the greeting. This is not a common term in the New Testament. Paul usually uses *eirēnē*, which means "peace," or in Hebrew *šalom*. This was the common greeting among Jews. Surprisingly James chooses the greeting commonly used in the Greek world, *chairein*, which, as we have said, is literally translated as "to be happy," "to be joyful."[2] Martin Dibelius asserts that James does this intentionally, for he wants to link *chairein* with *charan*, "joy," in the following verse, by the similar sounds. This literary device demonstrates the author's mastery of Greek.[3] From our hope perspective, we see beyond the literary device. From the beginning the author desires happiness, joy for those who suffer. This "catchword," which is linked with *charan*, a term that also means "joy," intensifies the author's wishes to bring a word of encouragement to the communities. Thus from the very first verse we note the joy-hope proposal that James brings to those who suffer oppression.

The Joy That Arises from Praxis

In 1:25 we note joy as a result of praxis:

> But the man who looks steadily at the perfect law of freedom and makes that his habit—not listening and then forgetting, but actively putting it into practice— will be happy [*makarios*] in all that he does.

The law of freedom is the law of service and is related to the "practical results" of 1:4. James refers to it as the royal law and sums it up in 2:8: "You must love your neighbor as yourself." John 13:17 says that those who wash the feet of others are happy. It is service that brings in joy. To say "will be happy" implies a certain ambiguity: happiness can be a future promise or it can be integral to the fulfilling of the will of God.[4] We should consider both interpretations correct, for they are not mutually exclusive. There is joy in serving and simultaneously the anticipated joy of the good that will come.

In James 5:10–11 we find the concrete example of the prophets and Job who were declared happy:

> For your example, brothers, in submitting with patience, take the prophets who spoke in the name of the Lord; remember it is those who had endurance that we say are the blessed ones. You have heard of the patience of Job, and understood the Lord's purpose, realizing that the Lord is kind and compassionate.

The example of the prophets clearly shows us the heroism of their position; because of their deeds they suffer oppression and martyrdom and because of those same deeds in defense of the oppressed and the weak they are declared blessed.

Job is an example of another kind of suffering person: It was not acts of denunciation that caused his misery, pain, and marginalization; rather he suffered innocently and arbitrarily. But he resisted and protested to the Almighty, and he was vindicated. It is noteworthy that in Job's case we see "the visible judgment of God which consists in the happy outcome of a period of suffering and not... in the reward of the next world."[5] When James asserts that God is compassionate and merciful, he introduces another element into the joy experienced in praxis, namely, the participation of God as a giver of joy. Joy in suffering is also paradoxically the result of the practice and the grace of God. Moreover, insofar as we know and affirm that God is compassionate and merciful, our hope is greatly nourished.

In the Letter of James we find numerous other occurrences of the word "joy," "pleasure," "happiness." In Greek the terms are *charan* (once, 1:2) and *makarios* (three times, 1:12,

1:25, and 5:11, the last time as a verb). In 1:2–4 the author writes:

> My brothers, you will always have your trials but, when they come, try to treat them as a happy privilege [*charan*]; you understand that your faith is only put to the test to make you patient, but patience too is to have its practical results so that you will become fully developed, complete, with nothing missing.

"Trials" here refers to the variety of oppressions and persecutions (*poikilois*) that produce suffering, not joy. At first glance the passage might surprise us with this *paradox,[6] for only masochists rejoice in pain. But James insists on infusing courage into his readers by making them reflect on their own bitter experience. In this verse the joy is not *eschatological, as Peter Davids would have it, the joy "of those expecting the intervention of God at the end of the age."[7] Nor is there any suggestion that people should rejoice in suffering per se. The author wants his readers to become conscious ("you understand...," *ginōscontes*) of the process and the result of that experience. It strengthens the spirit and forms a "militant patience," *hypomonēn* (of which we will speak in the next chapter), with fully developed works. All this bestows integrity on the person and on the community.[8] James is really talking about heroic deeds, for, as Dibelius says, he wants to revive the heroic sentiment of the period of the *Maccabees, who were oppressed by the Greeks.[9]

Anticipated Eschatological Joy

Beyond the joy that is experienced in service and the joy of hope despite suffering from oppression, there is an eschatological joy. This means knowing and believing that at the end of time the oppressed will be favored; therefore they rejoice in anticipation of that new order. James refers to that joy in a *beatitude of the eschatological type (1:12)[10] and in his

call to the downtrodden brother to glory in his exaltation
(1:9–11).

Let us consider the beatitude. James 1:12 says: "Happy
the one who stands firm when trials come. He has proved
himself, and will win the prize of life, the crown that the
Lord has promised to those who love him." This type of
beatitude used frequently by Jesus, especially in the Sermon
on the Mount, describes the attitude of the one who suffers as patience, resistance, and firm hope. Nonetheless, the
text does not emphasize virtue itself, but rather the promise of a new dawn, which is implicit in the initial "Happy
the one who..." and in the final promise of the crown of
life.[11] James, then, continues the idea begun in 1:2 ("Try
to treat them as a happy privilege..."), where he says that
the suffering community should reflect on the positive and
incomparable aspect of this experience that strengthens the
spirit. And he enforces it in 1:12 with this beatitude, recalling
the promise of the Lord. The purpose of all of this is to nour-
ish the hope of his readers. It is interesting to note that in
the beginning he addresses the whole group ("my brothers"),
and now he is addressing his readers at a more personal level
("happy the man [and the woman] who..."). Hope must be
real and total; it is achieved both through the community as
a whole that has hope, as well as on the individual level.

The trial referred to here is related to poverty, as Sophie
Laws suggests. The trial does not have to do with eschatological tribulation, but rather consists of a test linked with
poverty. Laws compares this text with 2:5, which speaks
of the poor as chosen heirs of the reign promised to those
who love God.[12] Laws is correct: there is a parallel that we
cannot ignore between "the crown of life promised to those
who love him" and "the reign promised to those who love
him." The latter phrase is clearly linked to the poor, and
the former, which we are analyzing, occurs immediately after
speaking of the poor and the rich. This relationship is not an
accidental one.

To have hope of winning the crown of life does not mean

entering into competition and winning, to the exclusion of others.[13] Rather it means *winning life itself,* good, lasting, eternal, different from the past. That is why they struggle for life, resisting, enduring oppression. This is the nature of their heroism and for it they receive the crown "of life," that is, life itself. It is precisely this hope in this new life that produces joy; if they endure their oppression courageously they can be sure that the crown is theirs.

There is, nonetheless, a new dimension to this passage: love for God. The text says that God has promised the crown to those who love God. If the passage ends in this way, we would expect it to begin "happy the one who loves the Lord for he will receive...." Or if we wished to emphasize the difference between those who endure the trial and those who love the Lord, we might read, "Happy the one who endures the trial and loves the Lord, because he will receive the crown of life." But James did not say it in this way, and to suggest that the final phrase responds to an *interpolation or a familiar cliché does not help much. James's expression has a meaning for us, namely, it identifies those who endure the trial with those who love the Lord. That is, they love the Lord; therefore they resist oppression.

Those who do not love the Lord do not endure the trial. The loving identification with the Lord strengthens hope and helps to overcome hostile situations. To love God is the other part of the "royal law" that James summarizes in 2:8: "You must love your neighbor as yourself." If James does not mention the two parts of the law together, it is because for him there is a very close relationship between the two; for as John says, if we say that we love God and we do not love our brother, we are liars (1 John 4:20).

Let us now consider the other eschatological joy that we find in the Epistle of James:

> It is right for the poor brother to be proud of his high rank, and the rich one to be thankful that he has been humbled, because riches last no longer than the flowers

in the grass; the scorching sun comes up, and the grass withers, the flower falls; what looked so beautiful now disappears. It is the same with the rich man: his business goes on; he himself perishes. (1:9–11)

Strictly speaking, this is not the same joy that we saw above. James uses here the term *kauchasthō,* "boast," "be proud," in its positive sense, which also connotes an element of anticipated happiness. This is a judgment pronounced beforehand in favor of the poor and against the rich. This judgment is, of course, common in Hebrew thought. The idea of the future reversal of the present unjust order was commonplace. Mary uses this idea in the Magnificat (Luke 1:52). It is to be expected, therefore, that James, an author writing in the context of oppression, should mention it.

There is an *antithetical structure between the brother in a lowly condition (*tapeinos*) and the rich (*plousios*); thus we cannot consider the humility of the brother a moral or spiritual characteristic. This is a brother who is economically poor, and he is lowly insofar as he is poor.[14] James is speaking to the poor of the Christian community (we consider it Christian because the term "brother" indicates that the poor person referred to is a believer, as most scholars agree). He tells the poor brother that he should rejoice from now on because his situation is going to change. He will no longer be humiliated but rather exalted. Interestingly enough, James does not say that he will be rich, but rather exalted, that is, raised up to the dignified level of a human person and recognized as a preferred creature of God.

The rich, on the other hand, will suffer the opposite fate; they will fail completely in their pursuits, namely, their business dealings, which are precisely the cause of their ruin since usually they are rooted in injustice and the desire for gain.[15] James is being sarcastic to the rich when he says that they should "glory" in their humiliation.[16] Later in the letter he says that they should begin to weep because of what awaits them. For now James leaves the rich no glimmer of hope:

not only their wealth will perish, but also their businesses and they themselves.

The Identification of God with the Poor

If the poor and oppressed know that God is in solidarity with them, loves them, and prefers them, their hope is greater. James reminds his readers of this, although the idea was well known. The God of Jesus Christ is the same who was known through liberating deeds on behalf of Israel and the poor in Israel, and God continues to defend the poor because in God "there is no such thing as alteration" (1:17). He tells them also that if the community is suffering this is not due to God, for God "does not tempt anybody" (1:13), and from God comes "all that is good, everything that is perfect" (1:17). The persons who are the cause of this situation of injustice are led by their concupiscence to sin and become murderers (1:15). Thus some kill and others die; some suffer poverty and others live luxuriously at the expense of their victims. In this conflict "the Lord is compassionate and merciful," says James, and hears the cry of the victims. For God "opposes the proud but he gives generously to the humble" (4:6).

The author of the epistle is very clear about God's affection for the outcast, for he places a *pagan prostitute, Rahab, on the same level as the patriarch Abraham. Rahab must have been scorned by the society of her day, for as a woman, a prostitute, and a pagan she had three strikes against her—and she would have problems today as well. Because of her hospitality to the messengers of Joshua, Rahab was justified. Although the figures of Rahab and Abraham appear together in other documents as models of faith, their juxtaposition still seems surprising. It is another indication of James's idea that there should be no favoritism in the community, for the result is always unfavorable to the poor.

The idea that there must be no favoritism within the Christian community does not imply that God is neutral or that God has no favorites. In this context God's partiality is clear: "Listen, my dear brothers: it was those who are poor according to the world that God chose, to be rich in faith and to be the heirs to the kingdom which he promised to those who love him" (2:5).

If favoritism is prohibited in the community it is because favoritism always favors the rich, never the poor. James forbids distinctions in this sense, not in the sense of favoring the poor, for that is what the Lord does.

The question of 2:5 is formulated in such a way that an affirmative response is expected. Thus we see that the community to which James addresses himself knows perfectly well about God's preference for the poor.

Here the poor are the *ptōchoi*, those who have absolutely nothing, not even a job; they depend on alms.[17] It is not true that James is here thinking of the poor as the devout or pious, as certain late rabbinic literature would have it. Many of the commentaries also follow this interpretation.[18] The context is very clear. Favoritism is being shown to the rich in a material sense, and the poor are being marginalized, oppressed (*atimaō*). And it is precisely the Christians, the supposedly devout, whom James is addressing. By this I do not mean that the poor are not pious, but only that if we make the poor and the pious synonymous then real economic oppression and God's concern for this very class of people are lost. The rich become the piously poor and the poor rich in piety, and the economic order and the unjust power stay as they are. Thus the rich always come out ahead: they are rich in real life and piously poor before God and thus the heirs of God's reign.

The approach to this text taken by certain scholars is suspect. James Adamson, a biblical scholar and a Presbyterian minister from the United States, for example, even before examining the text states, "not every rich man is doomed to be damned,...and not every poor man is sure to be saved."[19] This assertion is not striking in and of itself, since it could be made after analyzing the text; but it is striking that he

begins his analysis with this premise. His concern for the
rich and not for the poor is obvious; his readers are not of
the Third World. For his part, Leslie Mitton identifies the
poor with the devout and asserts that the term refers to "the
class of people for whom prosperity means little since obe-
dience to God means everything."[20] Only someone with a
job, food, and shelter could affirm such a thing. The hungry,
the exploited, the jobless want at least to satisfy their basic
necessities, and they turn to God with those hopes.

James refers here to the poor in both a concrete way and
in a general sense, not only to those who get no seat in
church and are treated badly.

It is worth recalling the uniqueness of God's preference for
the poor. This was unheard of and scandalous for other reli-
gions. In the Greek world, for example, there is no other god
who has this preferential inclination for the poor.[21]

These poor have been chosen by God to be rich in faith
and heirs of God's reign. But James does not define the meaning of faith in his letter, and so the crucial question becomes
more complicated: What does it mean to be rich in faith?
I think that it must have a very important meaning for the
poor. To be rich in faith cannot be relegated solely to a spiritual plane, completely disconnected from their situation of
poverty and suffering. To be rich in faith includes more than
being open to the Spirit with more naturalness than the rich.
It does indeed include being more sensitive to the presence
of God, but it includes something more: it means to hope
in the promise of God's reign. This is the reign inaugurated
by Jesus as he cured the sick, restored dignity to the outcast,
raised the dead. So to be rich in faith must be understood in
the same way as to be heirs of God's reign.[22] Reading this
text from the angle of hope we can imagine how much the
words must have meant for the oppressed.

This text leads us back to 1:12 ("Happy the man who
stands firm when trials come. He has proved himself, and
will win the prize of life, the crown that the Lord has promised to those who love him"). This appears to be a parallel

expression indicating that the poor are those who endure the test and that the crown of life is the reign promised to those who love God. A sign of the love of the Lord is, as we have said, the ability to resist oppression.

Having analyzed this text in which God is partial to the poor we might wonder about the rich. Is there hope for them in the picture that James presents?

In James 1:10–11 there is no hope, nor is there in chapter 5 (the judgment against them). It seems that there is, however, in 4:1–10. In that passage the author calls them to conversion, although he does not refer explicitly to them. If we read this text separately it seems that the call is a general one, but if we read the passages as an integral part of the letter we will realize that there are various signs that the rich are the intended readers, or at least those in the community who aspire to be rich. The three most notable signs are the tone, the absence of the vocative "my brothers," and the critique of idolatry.

When James addresses the community of believers, he always does so in an amiable tone, at times even one of supplication, which reflects solidarity with those who suffer and his concern to encourage and advise them. The tone of chapter 4 is radically different, harsh, very like that of chapter 5. He does not call them "my brothers," but rather "adulterers" and "sinners." To assert that this is due to the paraenetic style is not convincing, for even though it may be, the change is so radical that we must conclude that the words are not addressed to the same persons. Compare, for example, 4:1–10 with the following verse 11 addressed to the brothers.

James uses the vocative "my brothers" to address the community. When he addresses the rich he does not use it, not even when he refers to the merchants who probably do belong to the community (4:13–17).

As for his critique of idolatry, James criticizes in this chapter those who follow the impulses of their selfish passions and become friends "of the world," which for James means being an enemy of God. Most exegetes agree that James has in mind the words of Jesus about Mammon (the god of riches) and God, that is, two mutually exclusive masters. The theme of idolatry is present, the idolatry so strongly attacked by the prophets and regularly linked with the rich and the powerful. James calls them to conversion:

> Give in to God, then; resist the devil, and he will run away from you. The nearer you go to God, the nearer he will come to you. Clean your hands, you sinners, and clear your minds, you waverers. Look at your wretched condition, and weep for it in misery; be miserable instead of laughing, gloomy instead of happy. Humble yourselves before the Lord and he will lift you up. (4:7–10)

There is hope for the rich, but this is the only text in James where we see it. The condition is clear: they must be converted, that is, they must radically change their lives and purify their hands (of unjust business practices). In other words, they must cease being rich, for the rich for James are those who oppress, who exploit, and who blaspheme the name of the Lord. We must recognize that in the text of James, the rich are a stigma, just as the poor (*ptōchos*) are for an unjust society.

Judgment, the Hope of the Poor

Finally let us look at the last detail of the picture that we are considering from the angle of hope: judgment. It is not enough for James to infuse joy into the communities and remind them of the special love that God has for the poor. He wants also to assure them of the end of their oppression and suffering. He does this through judgment against the rich and proclamation of the imminent coming of the Lord. This is the strongest part of the letter. Just as the rich person, in the case of the landowner, had no mercy on the peasant, neither will James have mercy on the rich; he vents all his just fury. The style is apocalyptic; it recalls the judgment against Babylon the Great (Rome) and its very wealthy and powerful citizens in the book of Revelation (chap. 17):

> Now an answer for the rich. Start crying, weep for the miseries that are coming to you. Your wealth is all rotting, your clothes are all eaten up by moths. All your gold and your silver are corroding away, and the same corrosion will be your own sentence, and eat into your body. It was a burning fire that you stored up as your treasure for the last days. Laborers mowed your fields, and you cheated them—listen to the wages that you kept back, calling out; realize that the cries of the reapers have reached the ears of the Lord of hosts. On earth you have had a life of comfort and luxury; in the time of slaughter you went on eating to your heart's content. It was you who condemned the innocent and killed them; they offered you no resistance. (5:1–6)

We note how the transition from the prophetic to the apocalyptic style is made with no break, for the tone is undoubtedly prophetic in its denunciation of injustice but framed within apocalyptic judgment. The basic intention is not that the oppressed should see the suffering of the rich and rejoice in their sadistic feelings. The author wants his readers first of all to see the end of oppression. Thus this judgment against the rich is the most convincing hope for the poor. And there is no better way to express this than through the apocalyptic style. According to New Testament professor Horacio Lona:

> The apocalyptic style involves a hope determined by the certitude that an act of God in history will put an end to the present time and world and will bring in a new earth where the elect will enjoy salvation. This form of hope presupposes that in the present status of the world there is no possibility for salvation.[23]

Note how James simultaneously denounces injustices and announces their end. In 5:1 he calls on the rich to howl over the misfortunes that are coming upon them soon, and in 5:4, 6 explains the reason: exploitation, robbery, death. This hope for the end of oppression is not only for the members of the Christian communities, but for the oppressed workers in general. Likewise, the judgment against the rich does not specify whether they are Christian or not, although by the context of the letter it is clear that James does not consider such people to be Christians.

Later James reinforces the present hope, insisting that "the Lord's coming will be soon.... The Judge is already to be seen waiting at the gates" (5:8–9). There are other indications that for James judgment means hope for the end of oppression and the outcry of the poor. In the Bible, as Mexican biblical scholar José Porfirio Miranda demonstrates so well, the Last Judgment signifies the proclamation of justice for the poor and oppressed.[24]

– *Four* –

The Angle of Praxis

In situations of oppression like that experienced by the communities of the Epistle of James, hope, as we have said, is fundamental. Without it life would be nearly impossible. Nonetheless, hope is not sufficient; there is also a need for *praxis,* deeds. "Praxis" is a Greek word used in Latin America to express a liberating practice always linked to a transforming belief. James calls the communities to praxis, to make themselves felt in their environment by their testimony. For James, it seems, Christians are recognized not by their *being* but by their *doing;* by their fruits they are known. Here we will take the angle of praxis, following the lines delineated by James in his letter.

This is the sharpest angle. James writes with a heavy pen here. We can see that he is truly concerned about the life of the Christian communities. He wants them to be signs of God's reign. There are many details in the picture as seen from this angle, but they can be focused on three challenges that James makes to the communities: militant patience, integrity, and effective prayer. We can also see that the undergirding for these challenges is the unconditional and sincere love among the members of the communities, and beyond. Neither patience nor integrity nor prayer makes any sense if it is not motivated by love for others. Of the three challenges it is integrity that James focuses on the most. As we shall see, many of the details of the letter relate to this concern.

Militant Patience

For James one of the most important elements at the core of praxis is patience, a difficult attribute in desperate situations of oppression. Thus James insistently challenges his readers to "have patience."

Traditionally the word "patience" has been understood as signifying a passive and submissive attitude. People are patient because nothing can be done about their situations. Such an interpretation has been prejudicial for the lives of Christians and their communities, for it encourages resignation, a lack of commitment to concrete realities, and a subjection to the governing authorities (Rom. 13:1). James is not referring in any way to this kind of patience. He calls for a militant patience, that is, a very active and heroic patience, one that watches for the propitious moment. There are four Greek terms for patience: *anechomai, kartereō, *makrothymia,* and *hypomonē.* These are strictly military terms and are used as metaphors referring to the battles of life.[1] The author of the epistle uses two of these four Greek terms to refer to patience: *hypomonē* and *makrothymia.* Although these can be used synonymously, they have significant differences. *Hypomonē,* or the verb form *hypomeno* (used frequently in military situations), appears in the following contexts:

> ...you understand that your faith is only put to the test to make you patient [*hypomonēn*], but patience [*hypomonē*] too is to have its practical results so that you will become fully developed, complete, with nothing missing. (1:3–4)

> Happy the man who stands firm [*hypomonei*] when trials come. (1:12)

> ...remember it is those who had endurance [*hypomeinantas*] that we say are the blessed ones. You have heard of the patience [*hypomonēn*] of Job.... (5:11)

Here to be patient means to persevere, to resist, to be constant, unbreakable, immovable. Most scholars agree that there is an active meaning to the term.[2] James is very clear in this regard when he says in 1:3–4 that patience is accompanied by perfect works.[3] This is a militant patience that arises from the roots of oppression; it is an active, working patience. In 1:12 James speaks of those who resist the trial and overcome it, those who do not succumb to pain and oppression. This is heroic suffering, as Dibelius calls it. In the book of Maccabees, which narrates the Jewish resistance to the Greeks, the word *hypomonē* appears more than in any other book of the Hebrew Bible. In those accounts it speaks of "the courage and the patience [*hypomonē*] of the mother of the heroes and their children" (4 Macc. 1:11).

In the book of Revelation the word also continually appears with this same meaning. There the author speaks to us of the bloody persecution of the Christians and of the patience and endurance of the victims. According to Falkenroth and Brown, *hypomonē* frequently expresses the attribute of the person living in the light of the last days and is linked very closely to hope.[4] In Romans 5:3 we can verify this relationship. James 5:11 alludes to the patience (*hypomonē*) of Job, a personality often very mistakenly interpreted in our time. Here we have to understand "patience" in the same sense that we have seen. The patience of Job was in no way passive.[5] Only in the early moments of his miserable life was there any indication of resignation, but from chapter 3 on all his verbal fury erupted against his situation and he did not desist until the Almighty came onto the scene. Job did not succumb to pain; on the contrary, the more he experienced attacks, isolation, and suffering, the more he was strengthened, the greater his self-confidence. Job resisted unto death and God vindicated him.

This is the kind of patience that James recommends to the Christian communities. He may well have realized the difficulty of their situation and the need for valiant perseverance, that is, militant patience. Nonetheless, at the end of his letter

James employs the word *makrothymia* for patience, which
can be understood as a synonym for perseverance or persistence only in 5:10–11. On the other occasions the word has
a special nuance, namely, not to despair, to contain oneself,
to await an event that is sure to come. The term appears in
the context of the coming of the Lord and Judge.

After his furious attack against the rich in chapter 5 James
continues:

> Now be patient [*makrothymēsate*], brothers, until
> the Lord's coming. Think of a farmer: how patiently
> [*makrothymōn*] he waits for the precious fruit of the
> ground until it has had the autumn rains and the spring
> rains! (5:7)

> You too have to be patient [*makrothymēsate*]; do not
> lose heart, because the Lord's coming will be soon. (5:8)

> For your example, brothers, in submitting with patience
> [*makrothymias*], take the prophets who spoke in the
> name of the Lord. (5:10)

This term for patience does not have an active meaning
like the one we saw previously, but neither is it passive in the
traditional negative sense. The attitude is that of awaiting,
as it were, on alert. The farmers await with patience and joy
the fruit that will come from the care of their plants. They
can do nothing to make it come sooner, for everything takes
time. So too the oppressed community of James knows that
its difficult situation is going to change, that judgment has
been pronounced in favor of those who suffer. It is important then that they do not despair but that they "continue to
sow" and "cultivate the seedlings," which for James means
that they should follow the law of freedom and live a life of
integrity.[6]

The fact that James uses the word *makrothymia* for patience does not mean that we should wait for God to come
and do away with the oppressor. Davids promotes this pas-
sivity: "Patience, not resistance, is the virtue of the poor, for

their hope is the *parousia."[7] Rather it is a question of doing everything possible not to despair in spite of the desperate situation, relying on the future that will put an end to the sufferings.

In sum, from this angle of praxis we see that James calls the communities to have a militant, indomitable patience that awaits opportune moments.

Integrity

For James, the core of praxis is integrity, that is, consistency in hearing, seeing, believing, speaking, and doing. This is a personal integrity and a communal integrity. For James the churches should be signs of God's reign, a model different from the values of the world. At a time when there are many poor, the landowners take advantage of the workers, the merchants plot to earn more money, and the Christians are marginalized and dragged before the courts, the church out of concern for self-preservation runs the risk of imitating the values of that corrupt society. Therefore James exhorts them not to show favoritism toward the rich, not to seek the important places in the church (2:1), not to be envious, jealous, argumentative, not to be hypocrites speaking badly of one another.

For James and his community, Christians should be persons of integrity, sincere, transparent, consistent in everything they do. They should be sure of themselves, resolute, decisive. The author rejects shilly-shallying, for a community with indecisive members is doomed to failure. We see in the epistle great importance placed on unity among the members of the Christian community. This is a unity that helps strengthen them to confront a situation hostile not only to them as Christians but also to other poor people who have no one to defend them. It seems that for James unity arises from integrity, and God is the model of that true unity. The integrity of the Christians is demonstrated by their spiritual practice, which is pure and untainted before God the Father if it both practices justice and does not follow the values of this world (1:27). Let us look more closely at this core of praxis.

Integrity, Fruit of Painful Experience

From the beginning of the letter James introduces and focuses on the theme of integrity. After the greeting he makes explicit the process: joy, patience, tenacity, good and complete works, and the maturity that is the result, namely, to be complete and have integrity:

> My brothers, you will always have your trials but, when they come, try to treat them as a happy privilege; you understand that your faith is only put to the test to make you patient, but patience too is to have its practical results so that you will become fully developed, complete, with nothing missing. (1:2–4)

In his eagerness to encourage the Christian communities James asks them to reflect on the positive side of the experience of oppression. He does not perceive the recompense for this unjust suffering at the end of time; rather it occurs now, in the heart of praxis, in the life of the communities; they experience wholeness and integrity within themselves. Paradoxically this is a humanizing process. In the very process of resisting dehumanizing forces, the communities and their members are humanized.

The experience of feeling perfect (*teleios*), which in James means complete, total, should remind those who suffer that they are human beings, not things. In their experience of acute pain they should be able to integrate, within themselves, their flesh and their minds, their bodies and their souls. And because in this process the pain is almost palpable, the sensitivity of those who suffer to others who suffer is quite natural. Integrity, then, does not occur only in the body of one member of the community, but rather in the entire community, in which everyone becomes sensitive to the pain of the others within the community and outside of it.

To feel what the other feels is truly a gift that should cause
us to rejoice.

Integrity vs. Duplicity

James is against the two-faced person, or, as he puts it,
the person living a double life. He uses the term *dipsychos*
on two occasions, and he gives it a negative value. This is
the divided person, as distinguished from the "simple" person. The Greek *haplous* can also be translated as "open,"
"without ulterior motives"; the adverb *haplōs* means "unam-
biguously," and the adjective *haplotēs* "singleness of heart"
or "pure of heart."[8] In the Hebrew Bible, *dipsychos* corresponds to the phrase "with divided heart" (literally, "with
heart and heart"), which appears in Ezekiel 14:3–5 referring
to idolatry. The two instances where *dipsychos* appears are
1:8 and 4:8:

> That sort of person, in two minds [*dipsychos*], wavering
> between going different ways [*akatastatos*], must not
> expect that the Lord will give him anything. (1:8)

This text refers to those who pray with vacillation, with
hesitancy. James says that they are like the waves of the
sea moved this way and that by the wind. Such people are
a problem for the community principally because no one
can trust them, because they are both with the community and not with it. Moreover, they have no willpower,
no decisiveness. With such members of the community the
battle against oppression is lost. The word "wavering," "in-
constant," *akatastatos,* intensifies the unstable quality of
the ambiguous person. In praxis ambiguity, fickleness, and
instability are highly destructive.

> Clean your hands, you sinners, and clear your minds,
> you waverers [*dipsychoi*]. (4:8)

This exhortation is addressed to those who tend to make
friends with the world, or, in other words, to follow the values of the corrupt society described by James. Scholars agree

that this passage refers to idolatry: the friend of the world is the friend of Mammon, the god of wealth[9] and is therefore the enemy of God (4:4), for you cannot obey and worship two lords. Following this line of thought, 4:8 calls for integrity. These "adulterers," as James figuratively calls them, live a double life, are two-faced, are *dipsychoi*. Therefore he says that they must be purified, must clean their hearts and their hands. To clean one's hands means to cease doing evil,[10] to desist from corruption. James is probably alluding to certain members of the community who lived in a more or less comfortable situation and were driven by acquisitiveness, like the merchants in 4:13–17.

For James, then, you cannot live in ambiguity nor live two different lives. Either you believe that God generously answers prayers or God does not. Either you make friends with God or with the unjust world. Either you are in the community or you are out of it. A decisive option must be shown in praxis.

God, the Model of Integrity

James's understanding of God is closely linked to his concept of integrity. In James 1:5 God's attributes are contrasted with those of the divided (*dipsychos*) and fickle person:

> If there is any one of you who needs wisdom, he must ask God, who gives to all freely [*haplōs*] and ungrudgingly; it will be given to him.

The term to give "freely" is the translation of *haplōs,* "simply," "without second thoughts," a term opposed to *dipsychos,* as we have seen. The term *haplōs* can mean "to give without reservation," "sincerely," to give of oneself generously and without hesitation.[11] For God gives disinterestedly to the needy who ask. James intentionally introduces both opposing words to indicate that we should act as God acts. This line of thought continues in 1:17:

> it is all that is good, everything that is perfect, which is given us from above; it comes down from the Father of

all light; with him there is no such thing as alteration, no shadow of a change.

As in 1:5 he again alludes to what comes from God. He employs an illustration from astronomy. The God of all lights neither changes nor is changed by the shadow of rotation. Since God is the giver of good things, then, God never sends evil. God is faithful to God's own self and to God's children, born by God's own will with the Word of Truth (1:18). God, therefore, is a God of integrity; God is not two-faced or wavering, like the person in 1:8. This dependability of God is insisted on by Sophie Laws.[12]

But to know that God acts with integrity and then not to act like God is useless. This brings to mind 2:19–20: "You believe in the one God—that is creditable enough, but the demons have the same belief, and they tremble with fear. Do realize, you senseless man, that faith without good deeds is useless."

It has been said that in this text James refers to the classic formula for monotheism, that is, the belief in one God. Be that as it may, the close link between unity and integrity is clear. According to James, God is *one* not only because there are no other gods like God, but because God acts consistently with the divine purpose, which for James is the cause of the poor. The demons are frightened by this integrity of God, for God has been their steadfast enemy.[13] And since God does not change (1:17), the demons tremble.

Therefore, and here we come to the core of integrity, James challenges the communities to show their faith through works, for only in this way is the integrity of Christian life demonstrated. It is clear that James elaborates little theology in his letter and makes continuous reference to Christian practice. Nonetheless we must insist that his principal concern is not the general lifestyle of the communities, but rather, as Peruvian pastor Donato Palomino says, "the theoretical-practical unity of biblical faith for discipleship, where he contrasts the character of the militants with the structures of the system,"[14] that is, with the economic, political, and religious system of his time.

Faith and Practice, the Core of Integrity

For James, the link between the experience of oppression and eschatological hope is the practice of faith. At the end of the first chapter he summarizes the meaning of the spiritual life acceptable to God: "coming to the help of orphans and widows when they need it, and keeping oneself uncontaminated by the world" (1:27). The orphans and the widows, as we have pointed out, represent the oppressed and exploited, and the world responsible for their being oppressed represents the institutions, the structures, the value system that promote injustice or are indifferent toward it.

The Christian communities, then, must avoid accommodation to this unjust world and not fall into the trap laid by its value system. This, it seems, is what has occurred with some of the members of the community mentioned in chapter 2, which speaks against favoritism toward the rich and disrespect for the poor. Rather, the Christian communities should demonstrate the new values of justice, assisting the oppressed who are outcast from society.

James links practice with the law of freedom, faith, and wisdom. These three, which could be considered in a theoretical way, are effective and alive only insofar as they are demonstrated in the practice of justice; otherwise they are false and dead. James challenges the community to hear the word and keep it, to contemplate the perfect law of freedom and practice it, to speak and act consistently, as befits those who are to be judged by the law of freedom. He is not referring here to rites but rather to the *mišpatim* ("righteousness"), the laws of the ethical tradition of Sinai. According to 2:8, the law consists in loving our neighbors as ourselves; the other commandments, then, must be understood in relation to this one.

With regard to the law of freedom, James exhorts his readers:

But you must do what the word tells you, and not just
listen to it and deceive yourselves. To listen to the word
and not obey is like looking at your own features in
a mirror and then, after a quick look, going off and
immediately forgetting what you looked like. (1:22–24)

"Word," for James, means the perfect law of freedom (1:25).
Those who only hear the Word, without practicing it, demonstrate a lack of integrity; they deceive themselves. If it is
only heard, the Word loses its power, because it is only in
fulfilling the Word that it takes on life and is verified as true.
Yet, if those who hear it practice it steadfastly, says James,
the practice itself will be a cause for joy, for it is a sign of
consistency, integrity. Integrity as a cause for joy is referred
to in 1:2–4.

In 2:12 James says:

Talk and behave like people who are going to be judged
by the law of freedom.

These words occur in chapter 2, where James also speaks
against the lack of respect for the poor and the adulation of
the rich. The law of freedom is a unity; you cannot fulfill one
part of it and not another. If you do not commit adultery but
do show favoritism against the poor, you have transgressed
the royal law that "you must love your neighbor as yourself" (2:8–11). If the law of freedom is not fulfilled in its
entirety, it is not fulfilled at all. Thus the author challenges
his brothers and sisters to live with consistency and integrity
in their words and deeds; if they have made a decision to
obey the law of freedom they should act accordingly. If God
chooses the poor to be rich in faith and heirs of God's reign,
the brothers and sisters of faith should show a preference for
the poor over the rich, rather than favoring the rich, as it
seems that some were doing in the congregations.

After the description of discrimination, James continues
in chapter 2 with his concern for integrity, situating faith
and works together in a complementary unity. From a theo-

logical point of view, this is the most polemical part of the letter, for he seems to be contradicting Paul's view of justification by faith alone. In 2:24 James says: "You see now that it is by doing something good, and not only by believing, that a man is justified." This, together with the example of Abraham that he uses, leads us to believe that James knew well the expression "justification by faith." Some hold that it had become a slogan and that what Paul had meant was being distorted.[15] For some, justification by faith meant having faith without a commitment to others, without works. James, then, is trying to correct this idea by introducing works as an important element in justification.

We do not know exactly what James understands by faith, but he does make very clear what he understands by works. Throughout his letter he refers to the good works continually spoken of in the Gospels as the liberating deeds of Jesus; they are deeds that effect justice. They are the social works that the prophets demand and that are spoken of in the Sinai tradition. Paul, on the other hand, assails that law or system that is followed blindly and enslaves. For Paul the Christian must be guided by grace and faith. At no time does he place the works of justice in opposition to justification. Rather he says they are the fruits of the spirit that are born of faith.[16]

There is nevertheless a clear difference in the two approaches; this difference can perhaps be explained by the two different contexts. For James, faith cooperates with works, and through works faith achieves *perfection (2:22). Works justify therefore together with faith (2:24). In Paul the justified is the person who does justice because he or she is guided by faith and not by the law, system, or tradition that enslaves. The problem arises when we ignore the context of the passages. The intention of James, in the first instance, is not to speak about justification. He mentions this only in passing, probably because of misunderstandings of the Pauline phrase "justification by faith." From our angle of praxis we see that James wanted to emphasize the unity between faith and works as part of the necessary consistency in believing, hearing, saying, and doing. So he begins his reflection with a concrete example linking faith with the practice of justice:

> Take the case, my brothers, of someone who has never done a single good act but claims that he has faith. Will that faith save him? If one of the brothers or one of the sisters is in need of clothes and has not enough food to live on, and one of you says to them, "I wish you well; keep yourself warm and eat plenty," without giving them these bare necessities of life, then what good is that? Faith is like that: if good works do not go with it, it is quite dead. (2:14–17)

As we can see, James holds to his concern for integrity, consistency between theory and practice. What is new in this section is the importance for justification that he gives to "doing." For many who misinterpret the classic doctrine of justification this is scandalous, and for that very reason we should study all the more James's contribution to the doctrine of justification by faith. Like James, we must recognize that faith without works is dead (2:26).

Finally, James also links wisdom with works. We have seen the Word (or the law of freedom) and faith given life by works. Some have said that wisdom here means the Spirit,[17] as can be seen by the fruits mentioned in 3:17. If this is the case, we can see in James a systematic relationship between the Word, faith, and the Spirit as elements that, together with praxis, make up true Christian life.

James links wisdom with integrity in both contexts where wisdom appears. In the first (1:5), he says that those who lack wisdom should ask for it from God. He refers to those who have not achieved complete integrity, those who lack something. The verb "to lack" (*leipō*) makes the link. Wisdom, then, is important for integrity. All the following verses, as we have seen, speak in one way or another of consistency. James speaks of wisdom in 3:13–18 as well. Here he says that there are two kinds of wisdom, that from on high and the demonic. They produce different fruits. So those who think they have wisdom will have to show it by their works. These will reveal if their wisdom is true or false:

> If there are any wise or learned men among you, let them show it by their good lives, with humility and wisdom in their actions. But if at heart you have the bitterness of jealousy, or a self-seeking ambition, never make any claims for yourself or cover up the truth with lies—principles of this kind are not the wisdom that comes down from above: they are only earthly, animal and devilish. (3:13–15)

This text relates to 3:1, where he speaks of the problem in the community when many want to be teachers.[18] Perhaps it is these who claim to have wisdom. James insists that they show their wisdom through their good works and then it will be known if their wisdom is from on high or not. If it is, their wisdom will be pure, peacemaking, kindly and considerate, compassionate, bearing good fruits, without hypocrisy (3:17).

Integrity and Personal Honesty

Personal honesty, *transparency among the members of the community, is fundamental to praxis. James indicates this several times by the way he speaks. In chapter 3 he devotes considerable space to the abuses of the tongue and how difficult it is to control. Integrity is easily broken by the tongue (3:2): "We use it to bless the Lord and Father, but we also use it to curse men who are made in God's image" (3:9). James believes that this should not be the case, for both blessing and curse should not come from the same mouth (3:10). Those who consider themselves religious but do not control their tongues and so deceive their own hearts have the wrong idea of religion (1:26). On two occasions James exhorts the members of the community not to speak badly of each other and not to complain among themselves. In both cases he refers to the Judge, who can be either God or Jesus, as the only one with the right to judge (4:11–12, 5:9). For the good of the community the members should speak sincerely to one another and avoid all whispering behind each others' backs, for this wreaks destruction in the very heart of the congregation.

If the communities to which James is speaking are discriminated against and oppressed from the outside, they must strengthen themselves from within and not allow themselves to be undermined by internal divisions and misunderstandings. They must be transparent and sincere with each other. This is how we should understand 5:12: "Above all, my brothers, do not swear by heaven or by the earth, or use any oaths at all. If you mean 'yes,' you must say 'yes'; if you mean 'no,' say 'no.' Otherwise you make yourselves liable to judgment." That is, if total honesty is achieved in the community, it will not be necessary to swear, for what is said simply and without duplicity will be believed. This would mean that total personal and collective integrity had been achieved. Moreover, the community will act according to the circumstances: if someone is suffering, the community will pray; if someone rejoices, the community will sing; if someone is sick they will call the presbyters of the church to pray that the person be healed (5:13–14).

As we can see, integrity, in the sense of being consistent with oneself, with others, and with God, is a vital factor for praxis.

Genuine Prayer

For James prayer is a fundamental practice in the life of the Christian communities. It is mentioned several times in the letter. His insistence on the theme leads us to believe that James cannot imagine a Christian community that is not inspired by prayer, for it is through prayer that the Christian identity of these oppressed communities becomes visible. We have seen that James insists that his readers practice justice to be consistent with their faith in God. He also insists that this praxis be permeated and consolidated by a life of prayer, as an act of recognition, acceptance, and hope for the Lord.[19] In 1:6 and 4:3 James speaks of erroneous kinds of prayer. In the first case he refers to the person who prays with a duplicitous spirit (*dipsychos*). This is the two-faced person of whom we spoke in the previous section. It is impossible for this person to pray with faith because we cannot approach God with two hearts. The intimate encounter with God through prayer strips human beings and confronts them with their own selves. They experience moments of self-consciousness and self-criticism. This prayer is able to jolt and destroy the two hearts to create one heart, solid and honest.[20] Divided persons who want to pray with faith will be able to do so only insofar as they allow themselves to stand naked before God and become persons of simple hearts.

In James 4:3 he again mentions inappropriate ways of praying. James alludes to people with double hearts. They have two attitudes because deep down they look after only their own interests and not those of the needy. They bless the Lord and Father, but they also "curse men who are made in God's image" (3:9). They are not consistent with their faith; they do not know how to pray. James tells them that they must not expect that the Lord will give them anything (1:8), for "when you do pray and don't get it, it is because you have not prayed properly, you have prayed for something to indulge your own desires" (4:3).

Nevertheless, God is ready to listen to the prayers of others. In 5:4 God hears the cries of the mowers whose salaries were held back by the landowners. This is a spontaneous cry that arises from the hunger and pain of exploitation. It is a prayer that reveals the unjust inconsistency between what the landowners promised and what they actually paid. This bitter prayer is indeed heard by God; James 5:1–6 is part of the response to the workers' prayer.

Finally, and to conclude his letter, James dedicates several passages to the authentic practice of prayer. In 5:13 we see

the need for prayer in situations of suffering. We should dialogue with God in situations of oppression and violence, pain
and abandonment. Moments of prayer strengthen the spirit
and inspire us to the practice of liberation. Prayer gives us
confidence that God is present and accompanies these practices. Prayer also foresees moments of fullness in which we
feel the grace of God. The experience of joy is one such moment; therefore James recommends that psalms be sung, for
this will help make gratitude palpable.

James is concerned about communal prayer for the good
of all. He believes that it is necessary to join the power
of personal prayer to the prayer of others. Thus in situations like illness, we should rely on people who confirm
the power of prayer and the certitude that the Lord restores us in every way (5:13–15). It seems that the custom
was that "the elders of the church" fulfilled this function
(5:14). In this joint action we see that the leaders of the early
church were concerned about the well-being of the body,
and not only about spirituality. Prayer, then, strengthens us
in our suffering, gives fullness to our joy, and restores our
bodies.

There is a concern in the letter not to give the elders the
exclusive right to pray for others. In 5:16 he insists that
everyone should pray for others: "So confess your sins to
one another, and pray for one another, and this will cure
you."[21] In the overall context of our rereading of the letter, this passage takes on great meaning. Here the author
offers advice to the oppressed and disoriented communities,
some of whose members live with no consistency between
their faith and their works. He advises the mutual confession
of sins. This practice involves a process of self-criticism and
personal and communal purification. It requires enough humility to bow our heads to let another pray for us. It means
honesty and the confession of personal and collective sins,
without fear, with the freedom of love. It means opening
ourselves to our brothers and sisters in the same way that
we open ourselves to God in silent prayer. The community

that accepts this challenge will enter into the deep process of integrity to which it is invited.

The end of the letter emphasizes the power of fervent and constant prayer. James again insists that this is not the exclusive responsibility of the great leaders like the prophet Elijah, but that all the members of the community have this power. Elijah, says James, "was a human being like ourselves" (5:17), and his prayer was very powerful. In other words, the author challenges the communities to adopt the practice of prayer. Prayer will comfort them in their oppression, will exalt them in their hope, and will help them to achieve integrity in the practice of justice, as Christians faithful to God.

Five

An Open Letter to the Christian Communities

The Picture and Its Angles

We HAVE BEEN CONSIDERING THE PICTURE that James presents to us in his letter. Our analysis has surfaced three major concerns of the author. First is the situation of oppression that provides the background for the text. It is clear that the communities are experiencing oppression, marginalization, and perhaps persecution (2:6). At the same time the Christians are sensitive to the poverty and oppression of others, who are perhaps not Christian. James is greatly concerned about the suffering and thus writes his letter. It is clear from the form of the epistle that James wanted to make use of the teachings of Jesus; he frequently employs Jesus' sayings although he does not directly mention the name of the Lord.

The sufferings of the oppressed hurt James so much that he does not hesitate to denounce those who oppress others and steal their salaries, or those in the Christian community who out of weakness or opportunism become servile (2:1) or want to follow in the footsteps of the oppressors. James calls the oppressors rich (*plousioi*) and always refers to them in a negative way in the various contexts of the letter. He hurls all his fury at them in apocalyptic style. The author does not want to see the poor impoverished by the injustice of the rich any longer, and so he writes what I think can be called an open letter.

We have also viewed the picture from the angle of hope.

James feels the need to uplift the spirit of the communities, to give them enthusiasm and courage. The situation of oppression and pain tends to make people feel depressed, to dehumanize them, to destroy not only their bodies but also their spirit, to make them see their oppression as normal and natural. So James writes the letter to give them hope. God has created men and women for life. So they have to lift themselves up, to resist the pain of oppression, to confront the unjust reality, which is not normal and natural. God is on their side and against the oppressors. Rejoice now, for judgment against the rich marks the hope of the end of oppression.

And finally we considered the angle of praxis. Oppression and hope are united through deeds. There is an attitude that the poor should adopt in the face of oppression. First, they must have the assurance that God is with them, and hope provides this assurance. Then they must have militant patience, that is, of steadfastness, of resistance, of heroic endurance, all the while practicing justice. James also speaks of a patience that awaits the proper moment, as farmers await the harvest. They do not fall into despair, but rather wisely recognize the opportune moments. Prayer forms an integral part of this praxis. It shows us the close relationship we have with God in our deeds. Through prayer we ask God to act together with us in history. This is an active and powerful prayer that nourishes strength and certainty.

But James's greatest challenge to the Christian communities is integrity, consistency in all that we see, say, believe, and do. James rejects the *dipsychos*, that is, two-faced or two-hearted persons. These are the ones who are not consistent in what they believe and say, who know the law of freedom but do not follow it, who bless God and curse human beings, who belong to the community of faith but show favoritism against the poor, who ought to pay the workers' salaries but withhold them, who speak ill of others behind their backs, who see others in need but do not come to their material assistance.

For James Christians should above all show a consistency in their faith and their deeds. Their faith is alive only if it is accompanied by good works. And good works for James have to do with justice. So holiness or perfection (1:4) means being a person of integrity, wholeness, consistency. Religion pure and untainted before God is visiting and assisting the oppressed groups like widows and orphans and keeping oneself uncontaminated by the world, that is, not following the perverted values of society. Those who are friends of the world are enemies of God, for, as Jesus says, you cannot serve two masters.

The Epistle from the Underside

The Epistle of James has encountered many problems down through history. Its history is like that of documents intercepted because they fall under the suspicion of prevailing thought. James was not considered favorably because there was doubt whether he was the Apostle, the brother of the Lord. Apostolic authorship was a criterion for the inclusion of a document in the canon. He was also rejected because he does not speak enough about theology, especially Christology, as if Christian life had nothing to do with the theological task.

But the greatest objection to James, especially on the part of us Protestants, is that he overly emphasizes works, to the point that for James works collaborate in the perfection of faith, or complete faith. In these theological discussions we usually forget that the biblical writings emerge from particular historical situations. In the case of James the situation of oppression requires a praxis in the Christian communities that cannot be avoided by the formula of "justification by faith alone"—an affirmation of biblical faith that probably had been misunderstood (in the sense of opposing faith and works) and converted into a slogan.[1] James says no, because for him faith must show itself in justice, that is, in good works. Paul thinks no differently.

All these objections to James make us suspect that perhaps there is an underlying objection of a socioeconomic stripe. It would be interesting to know what the poor referred to in the letter thought. Did they have similar objections? It is noteworthy that in the Middle Ages there were great pilgrimages to Santiago (St. James) de Compostela in Spain. According to tradition, unproven but believed by the people, James, the brother of the Lord and the leader of the church in Jerusalem, had been in Spain. Great numbers of poor people participated in the pilgrimages, while the kings, the princes, and the rich went to Rome. Why did the poor prefer Santiago de Compostela?

It is also significant that the indigenous peoples of Guatemala make more images of James than of other better known saints. Why should this be? In many places throughout Latin America there is a common expression, *"Si Dios quiere"* ("God willing"). The source of the expression is attributed to James (4:15); how did such an expression become part of popular language?

We have seen that the letter has been interfered with, but it also must have had defenders. We know of some such as the radical reformer Andreas Karlstadt in the Reformation; he was very concerned about Luther's treatment of the letter.[2] The way the poor have read and received the letter throughout history is an important point for investigation in the future. This is, of course, a difficult task, for the poor have not written the official histories. But there are hints and these will help us rebuild this history from the underside.

The Crisis Caused by James

We said that we have "looked at" the picture painted by James, but this reading has been in no way passive. We have been engaged in an active reading of the letter because our eyes have looked at the present through the past and the past through the present. We have placed ourselves in solidarity with some persons and antagonized others. On the one hand, a reading in solidarity causes us simultaneously to suffer the pain and oppression of the persons mentioned in the letter, and to rejoice in the happy hopes that they experience. On the other hand, this identification is not strange or limited to persons and conditions of the past. In our day the oppression has intensified. Salaries are very low and often withheld. Racial and sexual discrimination is common. Who can deny that the *ptōchoi,* the poor, are many in the Third World and now, with economic globalization, in the whole world? So our reading of James cannot and must not be passive, but rather must be militant. James challenges Christians to be authentic, to respond as they should to the grace of God who lovingly has shown us the path of God's son Jesus Christ.

Nevertheless, we must recognize that a militant reading of James will cause a crisis for many Christians today. If we cast a self-critical look at our communities we will see that we are far from the ideal community proposed by James. Many of the defects attacked by James are to be found in our churches: favoritism, competition, gossip, hypocrisy, a dearth of just deeds, contentiousness. And if we look at the social class of our members we find that there are more from the upper middle class than there are poor. The rich in our congregations often take charge, and this is a story that is regularly repeated. Perhaps the problem—and this is difficult to deal with—is that for the author of the epistle the natural members of the congregation were the poor, and he excluded the rich.

This poses a question to our rich Christian brothers and sisters today and those who aspire to be rich. Why is it that from before the time of Constantine up until our day, the church has opened its doors to the rich and the rich have largely taken control of the church? This question concerning rich Christians is very serious and very complex. Christians who are rich and honest and seek to be in solidarity with the poor regularly ask it. The gospel response of "sell what you have and give it to the poor" is quite ingenuous today and does not respond to the structural complexity of society.

James indeed brings on a crisis for us, a painful but positive crisis. It is good that many poor people rejoice to find in James a friend who brings them good news, while others suffer a crisis of Christian identity, because James says that to be a Christian requires the fulfillment of certain conditions. The identity crisis that James causes for us is also a reason for joy. It can lead us to what James calls seeking Christian perfection, living with integrity, lacking nothing (1:4). John Wesley called this Christian perfection, or sanctification. This is one of the greatest challenges that James, and later Wesley, proposes to us.

John Wesley and the Letter of James

The Challenge of Christian Perfection

JOHN WESLEY, the founder of the Methodist Church, lived in the eighteenth century, and James, the author of the letter, lived in the first century. The times of James and Wesley and our own times are both very similar and very different. The experience of oppression and hope and the importance of praxis are alike, but our societies today are structurally much more complex. Styles of domination are much more sophisticated. False hopes abound; the ideological struggle is confronted directly. Today there is need for a praxis that takes into account the social sciences to analyze reality and act with maturity. In this light the importance of the Letter of James and the writings of John Wesley does not lie fundamentally in the "how" of praxis; they really do not contribute much in this regard, for their perspective is too narrow. It is up to us to fashion our own praxis. Their great contribution is rather the *emphasis* they put on praxis and the *implications of their proposals* understood in the light of our own contemporary situation.

With this in mind we can go on to analyze briefly what James and Wesley understand by "perfection." I am choosing this approach because it is the closest link between the two as well as their major concern.

First, both James and Wesley place great importance on good works. This concern is manifest in both their writings. It is interesting to note that both emphasize practice in response to misunderstandings of the doctrine of justification by faith alone, of Paul in the case of James and of Martin Luther in the case of Wesley. The *polemic can be detected as the background for their writings. For example, Wesley writes:

> Once more, beware of *solifidianism:* crying nothing but "believe, believe" and condemning those as *ignorant* or *legal* who speak in a more scriptural way.[1]

A little further on, Wesley refers to James 2:22: faith is made perfect by works. We find the same polemic in James 2, characterized by its diatribe style.

Neither James nor Wesley denies justification by faith; rather they simply insist that faith be made manifest in its complete form, for only then can it be considered truly alive. In a manner very close to that of James, Wesley describes authentic faith:

> For that faith which bringeth not forth repentance but either evil works or no good works, is not a right, pure and living faith, but a dead and devilish one.[2]

The way that they attempt to cover the gap caused by a radical separation of faith and practice is the notion of perfection; Wesley calls this Christian perfection, or sanctification. We will consider this idea in both James and Wesley.

The Letter of James places considerable emphasis on the idea of perfection. The word *teleios,* "perfect," appears twenty times in the entire New Testament; five appear in James. Moreover he uses the verb *teleō* twice and the substantive *telos* once. The adjective *teleios* comes from the verb *teleō,* which means "to complete," "to make perfect." Anything that has achieved its end is *teleios,* that is, perfect or complete.[3] The texts of the letter in which the concepts "perfect" or "perfection" appear are as follows:

In 1:4 James says "but patience too is to have its practical results [*ergon teleion*] so that you will become fully developed [*teleioi*], complete, with nothing missing." The meaning of *teleios* in this passage is "complete." The other terms, *holoklēroi* and *en mēdeni leipomenoi*, "with nothing missing," are explicative parallels of *teleion*. Those who are not perfect, mature, complete are the irresolute, the fickle, the two-faced (*dipsychos*).

In 1:25 James again uses the adjective *teleion*, this time to refer to the law, the perfect law of freedom. The use of "perfect" here indicates that the law is complete, it lacks nothing, and therefore it makes us completely free if it is carried out in practice.

In 2:8 James says that the royal law should be fulfilled completely (*teleite*), not only a part of it. If you show favoritism, you are not fulfilling the whole law. So, in sum, the law is perfect; it should be fulfilled in its totality, and we achieve perfection by hearing it and practicing it.

In 2:22 James emphasizes that faith and works form a single unit: "There you see it: faith and deeds were working together; his faith became perfect by what he did," that is, it is complete (*eteleiōthē*).

In 3:2 James relates *teleios* with the maturity reflected in self-control: "the only man who could reach perfection would be someone who never said anything wrong—he would be able to control every part of himself."

As we can see, in James the meaning of "perfect" is whole, finished, complete, mature. He is not referring to perfection in any absolute sense. According to Schippers, "When the term *teleios* is applied to ethics it does not denote the qualitative end point of human behavior, but rather the anticipation of the eschatological totality today. In the New Testament Christian life is not ideally projected as some struggle for perfection; rather it is seen eschatologically as the totality, both promised and given."[4] In fact, *teleios* can be applied in its fullest sense only to God and Christ. When it is applied anthropologically it refers to a person who has achieved maturity, an undivided totality of personality and behavior.

For his part, Wesley felt obliged to write a book that summarized everything he had said about Christian perfection, for there were many believers opposed to this doctrine. His work is entitled *A Plain Account of Christian Perfection.* (Interestingly enough, it is criticized by Argentinean theologian José Míguez Bonino because in it Wesley injects more of a note of individualism than he does in his other writings on perfection.[5])

Wesley begins his book by describing the influence of Anglican bishop Jeremy Taylor and the devotional writers Thomas à Kempis and William Law upon his doctrine. He says that they convinced him, on the one hand, that there is no middle way, or part of life, to dedicate to God, but that we must give of ourselves completely. And on the other hand, they convinced him that in our acts we should show a singleness of purpose in all that we say; only through such "simplicity of intention and purity of affection" can we ascend the mountain of God. Moreover there should be a single desire governing our character. In our religious practice, says Wesley, there should be a uniform following of Christ, a complete inward and outward conformity to our Master.

All this has to do with perfection, according to Wesley. Total love of God is the motivation for all acts of those who seek perfection. By loving God they love their neighbor as themselves. They become "pure of heart" with their only desire and purpose in life being to do God's will and not their own. Every thought that arises points toward God and is consistent with the law of Christ. These Christians are known by their fruits, and keep the entire law, not a part of it, nor even most of it, but all of it. To do this is a pleasure, "a crown of joy."

Wesley specifies that this is not perfection in the sense that there are no mistakes, ignorance, or other defects, but that these Christians are perfect in the sense of being free from evil desires. These are the "developed" Christians.

He argues that if the heart is evil, it gives rise to evil desires. But if we accept Christ, he purifies our heart. Perfection is achieved insofar as we have "the mind which was in Christ" and walk "as Christ also walked." On this basis Wesley asserts that the Christian does not sin, referring to 1 John: "Anyone who lives in God, does not sin" (3:6). This assertion, I believe, was what brought on the attacks on Wesley's doctrine. It seems that some felt it threatened the doctrine of justification by faith. Thus Wesley insists on separating Justification, or New Birth, from Sanctification, or Perfection. New birth leads the convert to a dynamic process of Sanctification or Perfection. This of course is not done separately from grace, for Wesley calls them gifts or blessings that must be acquired. He uses the words "sanctification" and "perfection" interchangeably. For example, he says that the perfect man is "completely sanctified." This is paradoxical, though, since elsewhere he says that there is no perfection in this world that does not allow for continuous growth.

Once perfection is achieved this does not mean that Christians do not "fall again." So Wesley provides advice for staying firm in this process of Christian sanctification. In sum, Wesley concludes that Christian perfection is the love of God and our neighbor and means freedom from all sin. It is received by faith alone. It is constantly given; it is finally achieved only in death. In several places in his writings he condenses his thought on perfection by saying that the perfect Christians are those who have faith, love, joy, and peace, and pray unceasingly, giving thanks for everything, bearing fruit in all their words and deeds. These are the Christians who are "mature in Christ."

Perhaps these contributions of Wesley would be of little significance if we did not look more deeply, taking into account his context, our own context, and the life of the churches. I believe we should thank Wesley for recovering works as part of faith. As Míguez Bonino says, "Wesley's struggle in defense of sanctification vindicates, I think, this active dimension of the life of believers and rejects any separation of faith and love."[6] Moreover, as Methodist theologian Theodore Runyon states, the notion of perfection in itself implies a rejection of the status quo and a tendency to change.[7] This provides the basis for rethinking this doctrine in the light of our own situation.

I think that the concept of Christian perfection in both Wesley and James is very similar, especially in that they both consider having achieved "perfection" those of integrity, without duplicity, consistent in their words and deeds. Nevertheless, their emphases are different. Wesley tends to relate everything to God and Christ and considers his hearers and readers as individuals. He emphasizes love of neighbor or good works as a result of total dedication to God. James, on the other hand, emphasizes more trans-individual relationships in the practice and demonstration of the faith. He tends more to "bring God down into history," to implement the law of freedom in everyday life, to show the favor of God to the poor and not the favor of human beings for God. James addresses himself first of all to the community and the relationships among its members. Again, this dimension is not absent in Wesley, as the personal dimension is not absent in James. But the emphases are different.

To return to our present situation: What does it mean to reach perfection? The word itself is abrasive, perhaps because in our societies we continuously seek out perfection, but of a kind radically different from that of James and Wesley. Our contemporary value systems are backward. For people today, perfection is linked to success, competition, excelling at the expense of others. For James it is the opposite; for him it is to attend to the needy in order to be consistent with what we believe and what we read in the Bible.

Perfection in our day casts aside the poor and those society wrongly calls handicapped. Perfection means having no defects. It is false because the world of appearances rules everything. In James perfection means authenticity, sincerity, while today it is appearances that matter. The models imposed by society are individualistic, leaving no room for solidarity. The image of perfection is provided; it means to be white, male, to aspire to economic success, good education, to have no physical defects, to be successful in all our activities, and to fall under no ideological suspicion. If such is the case the great majority of the poor and exploited are at a low level, a level of imperfection, because they never will have the opportunity to reach the image of perfection projected by our society. Our churches are not exempt from this false image.

James, and later Wesley, challenge us to seek another kind of perfection, authentic perfection. It is found in those who do not cause divisions among persons and communities, those who insist on integrity, completeness, wholeness, those who relate their situation to their faith and act with consistency in what they say and what they do. This is to be honest, and those who do not act in this way are dishonest. In our Christian communities we should reflect on this crucial aspect. And we should do this as well in all kinds of movements that attempt to transform our perverted social situation.

To be "pure of heart" means much more than to be a good person. The continuous quest for honesty today, understood in all its depth and situated at the center of our conflict-ridden history, will help us to be authentic Christians, for to be a person of integrity means to be honest with God, with our neighbor, with ourselves, and with our situation.

This is one of the greatest challenges that James presents to us today.

Notes

Chapter 1: The Intercepted Letter

1. See the discussion in James Hardy Ropes, *A Critical and Exegetical Commentary on the Epistle of St. James* (Edinburgh: T. & T. Clark, 1978); Martin Dibelius, *James*, rev. Heinrich Greeven (Philadelphia: Fortress Press, 1976); and Sophie Laws, *A Commentary on the Epistle of James* (New York: Harper & Row, 1980).

2. Wittenberg, 1522. In the preface to the second edition he omits the phrase "epistle of straw," but his opinion about the letter has not changed at all. See Laws, *James*, p. 1; Ropes, *James*, p. 106.

3. Donald Guthrie, *New Testament Introduction* (Downer's Grove, Ill.: InterVarsity Press, 1970), p. 736.

4. Dibelius, *James*, p. 54.

5. The parallels with the Sermon on the Mount and other sayings of Jesus are as follows:

1:2:	Joy in the midst of trials (Matt. 5:11–12)
1:4:	Exhortation to perfection (Matt. 5:48)
1:5:	Petition for wisdom (Matt. 7:7)
1:20:	Against anger (Matt. 5:22)
1:22:	Hearers and doers of the Word (Matt. 7:24)
2:10:	To keep the law in its entirety (Matt. 5:19)
2:13:	Blessed are the merciful (Matt. 5:7)
3:18:	Blessed are the peacemakers (Matt. 5:9)
4:4:	Friendship with the world as enmity toward God (Matt. 6:24)
4:10:	Blessed are the meek (Matt 5:4)
4:11, 12:	Against judging others (Matt. 7:1–5)
5:2ff.	Moths and worms that destroy wealth (Matt. 6:19)
5:10:	The prophets as an example (Matt. 5:12)
5:12:	Against oaths (Matt. 5:33–37)
1:6:	To ask with faith and without hesitation (Matt. 21:21)

2:8: To love one's neighbor as the great commandment
(Matt. 22:39)
3:1: On the desire to be called teacher (Matt. 23:8–12)
3:2: On the dangers of speech (Matt. 12:36, 37)
5:9: The divine Judge at the gate (Matt. 24:33).

We should clarify that the frequent parallel with Matthew does not imply copying but rather recollections of the oral teaching of Jesus. For his part, Davids points out the similarity with Luke. See Peter H. Davids, *The Epistle of James: A Commentary on the Greek Text* (Grand Rapids, Mich.: William B. Eerdmans, 1982), pp. 47, 48.

6. Wittenberg, 1522. See Ropes, *James,* p. 106.
7. Dibelius, *James.*
8. Davids, *James.*
9. Ibid., p. 182.
10. Laws, *James,* p. 41.
11. Ibid., p. 25.
12. Davids, *James,* p. 22.
13. Ibid., pp. 28–34.
14. Some believe that the letter was a Jewish document and that a few Christian interpolations were made later.
15. Of these, forty-five appear in the Septuagint (LXX), but thirteen are completely new in the Bible (Davids, *James,* pp. 58, 59).
16. For a more detailed analysis of the style, in addition to the introductions to the commentaries of Dibelius, Ropes, and Davids, see Anselm Schultz, "Formas fundamentales de la parenesis primitiva," in *Forma y propósito del Nuevo Testamento,* ed. Josef Schreiner (Barcelona: Herder, 1973).
17. Laws, Dibelius, Ropes, Adamson, and others.

Chapter 2: The Angle of Oppression

1. For example, see Martin Dibelius, *James*, rev. Heinrich Greeven (Philadelphia: Fortress Press, 1976).
2. Sophie Laws, *A Commentary on the Epistle of James* (New York: Harper & Row, 1980), p. 9.
3. Peter Davids, *Commentary on James* (Grand Rapids, Mich.: William B. Eerdmans, 1982), p. 30.
4. Contrary to what is asserted by Davids, ibid.
5. For a more detailed study see Thomas Hanks, *God So*

Loved the Third World (Maryknoll, N.Y.: Orbis Books, 1983), and Elsa Tamez, *The Bible of the Oppressed* (Maryknoll, N.Y.: Orbis Books, 1982).

6. Davids, *James,* p. 177.

7. James Adamson, *The Epistle of James* (Grand Rapids, Mich.: William B. Eerdmans, 1976), p. 186.

8. Joachim Jeremias, *Jerusalem in the Time of Jesus* (Philadelphia: Fortress Press, 1969), p. 111.

9. Adamson, *James,* p. 186.

10. Davids, *James,* pp. 177–78.

11. See, for example, Isa. 1:10–17; Deut. 14:29; 24:17–21; Ezek. 22:7; Zech. 7:10.

12. See Acts 6:1–6; 1 Tim. 5:3. See also Adamson, *James,* p. 86; Laws, *James,* p. 89; Davids, *James,* p. 103.

13. Laws, *James,* p. 89.

14. Hanks, *God So Loved the Third World,* pp. 44–50.

15. Ibid., p. 47.

16. In the *Interpreter's Dictionary of the Bible,* Supplementary Volume (Nashville: Abingdon Press, 1981), p. 470. This refers to the papyrus Bodmer 17 p74. See Laws, *James,* p. 90.

17. John H. Elliott, *A Home for the Homeless: A Sociological Exegesis of 1 Peter, Its Situation and Strategy* (Philadelphia: Fortress Press, 1981), pp. 21–58.

18. *"Ptōchos,"* Kittel, *Theological Dictionary of the New Testament,* 6:885.

19. *"Penēs,"* ibid., 6:37.

20. Wolfgang Stegemann, *The Gospel and the Poor* (Philadelphia: Fortress Press, 1984), p. 15.

21. This is not Stegemann's view; he says that there were no *ptōchoi* in the early Christian community; for him the community was made up of *penēs* and *penētes.*

22. For the most part James follows the LXX with this phrase. See Ps. 1:1, Prov. 8:34. But in the LXX we also find the term *anthrōpos: makarios de anthrōpos...* (Job 5:17).

23. Martin Hengel, *Property and Riches in the Early Church* (Philadelphia: Fortress Press, 1974), p. 15.

24. Jeremias, *Jerusalem,* pp. 95–99.

25. Apart from the tradition that is critical of riches, there is another, more common tradition in later Jewish thought; in it the poor are spiritualized and the term "poor" becomes synony-

mous with pious. Riches are then accepted as a gift of God. James
follows the former tradition.

26. Laws, *James,* p. 98.

27. Davids, *James,* p. 108.

28. Laws, *James,* p. 104.

29. Exod. 1:13; Deut. 24:7; 1 Kings 12:4; Hos. 12:8; Amos
4:1; 8:4; Mic. 2:2; Hab. 1:4; Jer. 22:3; Ezek. 18:7, 12, 16; 22:7;
45:8; 46:18.

30. Tamez, *Bible of the Oppressed,* pp. 32–33.

31. This is the term A. M. Hunter uses, as cited in Adamson,
James, p. 20.

32. For example, Wayne Meeks analyzes the Pauline communities and concludes that they were constituted by members of
different social strata, especially merchants and artisans. There
were persons of some wealth but with an ambiguous social status, often because they had been slaves. See Wayne A. Meeks, *The
First Urban Christians* (New Haven: Yale University Press, 1983),
pp. 72–73.

33. Hanks, *God So Loved the Third World,* p. 46.

34. Laws, *James,* p. 104.

35. Hengel, *Property and Riches,* pp. 64–65.

Chapter 3: The Angle of Hope

1. James Adamson, *The Epistle of James* (Grand Rapids, Mich.:
William B. Eerdmans, 1976), p. 52.

2. As documented in the papyri and other sources (Sophie
Laws, *A Commentary on the Epistle of James* [New York: Harper
& Row, 1980], p. 49).

3. Martin Dibelius, *James,* rev. Heinrich Greeven (Philadelphia:
Fortress Press, 1976), p. 68.

4. This idea was common in the tradition of the early church.
See 1 Pet. 1:6–7 and Rom. 5:2–5 (Peter H. Davids, *The Epistle of
James: A Commentary on the Greek Text* [Grand Rapids, Mich.:
William B. Eerdmans, 1982], pp. 65–66).

5. Ibid., p. 67.

6. Nor does Laws believe that there is an eschatological term
to the series of James; for Laws the trials lead to personal integrity,
an end in itself (*James,* p. 52).

7. Dibelius, *James,* p. 73.

8. Davids asserts that this is an eschatological saying (*James*, p. 100). Sophie Laws recognizes the ambiguity and thinks that it is probable that the author considers both interpretations to be correct (*James*, pp. 87–88).

9. Dibelius, *James*, p. 246.

10. According to Klaus Koch there are two types of beatitudes in the Bible: one appears in the wisdom literature of the Hebrew Bible as the conclusion to a series of prayers or a logical argument, and the other is the apocalyptic blessing directed to those who will be saved in the last judgment and participate in the new world because they have remained true to their faith. The blessing of James falls in the latter category (*The Growth of the Biblical Tradition* [New York: Charles Scribner's Sons, 1969], p. 7).

11. Ibid., p. 8.

12. Laws, *James*, p. 67.

13. Adamson, *James*, p. 67.

14. Laws, *James*, p. 62.

15. See Elsa Tamez, *The Bible of the Oppressed* (Maryknoll, N.Y.: Orbis Books, 1982), pp. 49–50.

16. This is the view of Dibelius and Laws, as opposed to others like Ropes and Adamson, who believe that the rich person referred to is a member of the Christian community because the word *adelphos*, they hold, refers to both the poor man and the rich man.

17. "*Ptōchos,*" Kittel, *Theological Dictionary of the New Testament*, 6:888.

18. Dibelius, Adamson, Davids, Mitton, etc.

19. Adamson, *James*, pp. 108–9.

20. Leslie Mitton, *The Epistle of James* (Grand Rapids, Mich.: William B. Eerdmans, 1966), p. 86.

21. "*Ptōchos,*" Kittel, *Theological Dictionary of the New Testament*, 6:887.

22. This is also the view of Davids, *James*, pp. 111, 112.

23. Horacio Lona, "L'attente et savoir de la fin apocalyptique et eschatologique neotestamentaires," *Lumière et Vie* 160 (1982): 27.

24. José Porfirio Miranda, *Marx and the Bible* (Maryknoll, N.Y.: Orbis Books, 1974), pp. 111–36.

Chapter 4: The Angle of Praxis

1. Colin Brown, *Dictionary of New Testament Theology* (Grand Rapids, Mich.: Zondervan, 1977), 2:764.

2. See Dibelius, Laws, Adamson, Davids, etc.

3. The term "perfect works" has been translated as "the patience that reaches perfection."

4. In Brown, *Dictionary,* 2:774.

5. I do not agree with scholars who hold that James had in mind the Job of the *Testament of Job* and not the canonical book of Job. The Job of the *Testament* is patient in the sense of passive resignation.

6. The term *makrothymia* has another meaning, even more common in the LXX and in other parts of the New Testament. In the Greek Old Testament it is used to refer to the patience of God. God is patient with human beings; God mercifully controls the divine anger to give human beings time to be converted and change their attitudes. In this case to have patience is to have mercy, to have clemency. In Romans 2:4 the patience of God leads us to conversion—*metanoia.* In the parable of the unjust steward, Matthew 18:23–35, this meaning is clearly seen. The steward asked for patience from the Lord (*makrothymia*) for his debt and promised to pay back everything. In his mercy the master pardoned the debt, which the steward did not do with his peers, and so ended up in jail. This connotation does not easily fit into our text of James, for the author indicates the meaning we should use with his example of the laborer.

7. Peter H. Davids, *The Epistle of James: A Commentary on the Greek Text* (Grand Rapids, Mich.: William B. Eerdmans, 1982), p. 181.

8. Kittel, *Theological Dictionary of the New Testament,* 1:386–87.

9. James Adamson, *The Epistle of James* (Grand Rapids, Mich.: William B. Eerdmans, 1976), p. 170.

10. Davids, *James,* p. 167.

11. Kittel, *Theological Dictionary of the New Testament,* 1:386–87.

12. Sophie Laws, *A Commentary on the Epistle of James* (New York: Harper & Row, 1980), pp. 49–61, 126.

13. Ibid., p. 126.

14. In his unpublished dissertation, "Paradigmas bíblicos para una pastoral obrera," San José, Costa Rica: Seminario Bíblico Latinoamericano, 1984, p. 145.

15. Laws, *James,* p. 131.

16. See Elsa Tamez, *The Amnesty of Grace* (Nashville: Abingdon Press, 1992).

17. See J. A. Kirk, "The Meaning of Wisdom in James: Examination of a Hypothesis," *New Testament Studies* 16, no. 1 (October 1969): 24–38.

18. See Davids, *James,* p. 149; see also Dibelius, *James,* p. 208.

19. Jon Sobrino speaks of "the necessity of prayer for discovering the meaning of Christian praxis within this praxis" (*La oración de Jesús y del cristiano* [Mexico City: CRT, 1981], p. 8).

20. Frei Betto believes that "prayer makes us more sensitive to the manifestations of institutionalized lies" (*Oração na ação* [Rio de Janeiro: Civilização Brasileira, 1977], p. 38).

21. It seems that James intentionally did not assign the elders the exclusive right to pray for others. This text and the example of Elijah suggest this.

Chapter 5: An Open Letter to the Christian Communities

1. Sophie Laws, *A Commentary on the Epistle of James* (New York: Harper & Row, 1980), p. 131.

2. George H. Williams, *La Reforma radical* (Mexico City: Fondo de Cultura Económica, 1983), p. 468; in Eng. see *Radical Reformation* (Philadelphia: Westminster, 1962).

Appendix: John Wesley and the Letter of James

1. John Wesley, "A Plain Account of Christian Perfection," in *John and Charles Wesley: Selected Prayers, Hymns, Journal Notes, Sermons, Letters and Treatises,* ed. Frank Whaling, Classics of Western Spirituality (New York: Paulist Press, 1981), p. 363.

2. "Of True Christian Faith," in *John Wesley,* ed. Albert C. Outler, A Library of Protestant Thought (New York: Oxford University Press, 1964), p. 128.

3. R. Schippers, "Goal," in *Dictionary of New Testament Theology,* ed. Colin Brown (Grand Rapids, Mich.: Zondervan, 1976), 2:59.

4. Ibid., p. 65.

5. José Míguez Bonino, "Justificación, santificación, y plenitud," in *La tradición protestante en la teología latinoamericana,* ed. José Duque (San José, Costa Rica: DEI, 1983), p. 254.

6. Ibid., p. 250.

7. Theodore Runyon, "Wesley and the Theologies of Liberation," in *Sanctification and Liberation,* ed. Theodore Runyon (Nashville: Abingdon Press, 1981).

Bibliography

Resources marked with an asterisk (*) are available from the General Board of Global Ministries, The United Methodist Church's Service Center; stock number (#) and price are listed for ordering. See p. 178 for complete ordering information.

Adamson, James B. *The Epistle of James*. New International Commentary on the New Testament. Grand Rapids, Mich.: William B. Eerdmans, 1976.

Barclay, William, ed. *Letters of James and Peter*. The Daily Study Bible Series. Rev. ed. Louisville: Westminster John Knox Press, 1976.

Bauckham, Richard J. *James: Wisdom of James, Disciple of Jesus the Sage*. New Testament Readings. London: Routledge, 1999.

*Beckmann, David, and Arthur Simon. *Grace at the Table: Ending Hunger in God's World*. New York: Paulist Press, 1999. #3428, $10.95.

Betto, Frei. *Oração na ação*. Rio de Janeiro: Ed. Civilização Brasileira, S.A., 1977.

Boff, Leonardo, and Clodovis Boff. *Introducing Liberation Theology*. Maryknoll, N.Y.: Orbis Books, 1987.

Bray, Gerald, ed. *James, 1–2 Peter, 1–3 John, Jude*. Ancient Christian Commentary on Scripture—New Testament. General editor Thomas C. Oden. Chicago: Fitzroy Dearborn Publishers, 2000.

Brown, Colin. *Dictionary of New Testament Theology*. Grand Rapids, Mich.: Zondervan, 1977.

Chester, Andrew, and Ralph P. Martin. *The Theology of the Letters of James, Peter and Jude*. New Testament Theology. Cambridge: Cambridge University Press, 1994.

Comblin, Jose. *Called for Freedom: The Changing Context of Liberation Theology*. Maryknoll, N.Y.: Orbis Books, 1998, $25.00.

Countryman, L. William. *The Rich Christian in the Church of the Early Empire: Contradictions and Accommodations*. New York: Edwin Mellen Press, 1980.

Davids, Peter H. *The Epistle of James: A Commentary on the Greek Text*. The New International Greek Testament Commentary. Grand Rapids, Mich.: William B. Eerdmans, 1982.

———. *James*. New International Biblical Commentary. Peabody, Mass.: Hendrickson Publishers, 1989, 1993.

*Dennis, Mark, Renny Golden, and Scott Wright. *Oscar Romero: Reflections on His Life and Writings*. Maryknoll, N.Y.: Orbis Books, 2000. #3448, $13.00.

de Santa Ana, Julio. *Good News to the Poor: The Challenge of the Poor in the History of the Church*. Maryknoll, N.Y.: Orbis Books, 1979.

Dibelius, Martin. *James*. Revised by Heinrich Greeven. Hermeneia. Philadelphia: Fortress Press, 1976.

*Dodson, Lisa. *Don't Call Us Out of Name: The Untold Lives of Women and Girls in Poor America*. Boston: Beacon Press, 1999. #3117, $16.00.

Elliott, John H. *A Home for the Homeless: A Sociological Exegesis of 1 Peter, Its Situation and Strategy*. Philadelphia: Fortress Press, 1981.

*Freeman, Richard B. *The New Inequality: Creating Solutions for Poor America*. Boston: Beacon Press, 1999. #3446, $11.00.

Gebara, Ivone. *Longing for Running Water: Ecofeminism and Liberation*. Trans. David Molineaux. Minneapolis: Fortress Press, 1999.

Gench, Frances Taylor, et al. *Hebrews and James*. Westminster Bible Companion. Louisville: Westminster John Knox Press, 1996.

*Gonzalez, Juan. *Harvest of Empire: A History of Latinos in America*. New York: Penguin USA, 2001. #3430, $14.00.

Guthrie, Donald. *New Testament Introduction*. Downers Grove, Ill.: InterVarsity Press, 1970.

Gutiérrez, Gustavo. *A Theology of Liberation: History, Politics and Salvation*. Maryknoll, N.Y.: Orbis Books, 1988.

———. *The Density of the Present: Selected Writings*. Maryknoll, N.Y.: Orbis Books, 1999.

Hanks, Thomas. *God So Loved the Third World: The Biblical Vocabulary of Oppression.* Maryknoll, N.Y.: Orbis Books, 1983.

Hanson, K. C., and Douglas E. Oakman. *Palestine in the Time of Jesus: Social Structures and Social Conflicts.* Minneapolis: Fortress Press, 1998.

Hartin, Patrick J. *A Spirituality of Perfection: Faith in Action in the Letter of James.* Collegeville, Minn.: Liturgical Press, 1999.

Hengel, Martin. *Property and Riches in the Early Church: Aspects of a Social History of Early Christianity.* Philadelphia: Fortress Press, 1974.

Hennelly, Alfred T. *Liberation Theologies: The Global Pursuit of Justice.* Mystic, Conn.: Twenty-third Publications, 1995.

The Interpreter's Dictionary of the Bible, Supplementary Volume. Nashville: Abingdon Press, 1981.

Jackson-McCabe, Matthew A. *Logos and the Law in the Letter of James: The Law of Nature, the Law of Moses, and the Law of Freedom.* Leiden and Boston: Brill, 2001.

Jeremias, Joachim. *Jerusalem in the Time of Jesus: An Investigation into Economic and Social Conditions during the New Testament Period.* Philadelphia: Fortress Press, 1969.

Johnson, Luke Timothy. *The Letter of James: A New Translation With Introduction and Commentary.* Anchor Bible 37A. New York: Doubleday, 1995.

———. *The Letter of James.* The New Interpreter's Bible. Nashville: Abingdon Press, 1998.

Keck, Leander, ed. *The New Interpreter's Bible.* Nashville: Abingdon Press, 1994.

Kirk, J. A. "The Meaning of Wisdom in James: Examination of a Hypothesis," in *New Testament Studies* 16, no. 1 (October 1969): 24–38.

Koch, Klaus. *The Growth of the Biblical Tradition: The Form-Critical Method.* New York: Charles Scribner's Sons, 1969.

Landes, David. *The Wealth and Poverty of Nations: Why Some Are So Rich and Some So Poor.* New York: W. W. Norton, 1998.

Laws, Sophie. *The Epistle of James.* Black's New Testament Commentaries. Peabody, Mass.: Hendrickson Publishers, 1980, 1993.

*Leonard, Ann, ed. *Seeds 2: Supporting Women's Work Around the World.* New York: Feminist Press, 1995. #3163, $12.95.

Living in a World of Wealth and Poverty: Managing Your Resources with Compassion and Integrity. Word in Life Priorities for Living Workbook. Nashville: Thomas Nelson, 1995.

Lona, Horacio. "L'attente et savoir de la fin apocalyptique et eschatolologie neotestamentaires" in *Lumière et Vie* 160 (1982): 25–33.

Maynard-Reid, Pedrito U. *Poverty and Wealth in James.* Maryknoll, N.Y.: Orbis Books, 1987.

Meeks, Wayne. *The First Urban Christians: The Social World of the Apostle Paul.* New Haven, Conn.: Yale University Press, 1983.

Míguez Bonino, José. "Justificación, santificación y plenitud" in *La tradición protestante en la teología latinoamericana.* Ed. José Duque. San José, Costa Rica: DEI, 1983.

Mitton, Leslie. *The Epistle of James.* Grand Rapids, Mich.: William B. Eerdmans, 1966.

Miranda, José Porfirio. *Marx and the Bible: A Critique of the Philosophy of Oppression.* Maryknoll, N.Y.: Orbis Books, 1974.

Moo, Douglas J., and D. A. Carson. *The Letter of James.* Pillar New Testament Commentary. Grand Rapids, Mich.: William B. Eerdmans, 2000.

Newsom, Carol A., and Sharon H. Ringe, eds. *The Women's Bible Commentary.* Louisville: Westminster John Knox Press, 1992.

Nolan, Albert, O.P. "The Service of the Poor and Spiritual Growth." In "The Dilemma of the '90s: Economic Injustice, Hunger and Hope in Latin America." *National Journal of the Chicago Religious Task Force on Central America* 2 (June 1991): 53–56.

Nystrom, David P. *James.* NIV Application Commentary. Grand Rapids, Mich.: Zondervan, 1997.

Palmer, Earl F. *The Book That James Wrote.* Grand Rapids, Mich.: William B. Eerdmans, 1997.

Palomino, Donato. "Paradigmas bíblicos para una pastoral obrera," Seminario Bíblico Latinoamericano, 1984.

Penner, Todd C. *The Epistle of James and Eschatology: Re-reading an Ancient Christian Letter.* Sheffield, Eng.: Sheffield Academic Press, 1996.

Perkins, Pheme. *First and Second Peter, James, and Jude.* Louis-
    ville: Westminster John Knox Press, 1995.

Ropes, James Hardy. *A Critical and Exegetical Commentary on
    the Epistle of James.* International Critical Commentary. Edin-
    burgh: T. & T. Clark, 1916.

Runyon, Theodore. "Wesley and the Theologies of Liberation."
    In *Sanctification and Liberation,* ed. Theodore Runyon. Nash-
    ville: Abingdon Press, 1981.

Russell, Letty, et al. *Human Liberation in a Feminist Perspective:
    A Theology.* Louisville: Westminster John Knox Press, 1995.

Schippers, R. "Goal." Page 59 in *Dictionary of the New Testament
    Theology.* Vol. 2. Ed. Colin Brown. Grand Rapids, Mich.:
    Zondervan, 1976.

Schreiner, Josef, ed. *Forma y propósito del Nuevo Testamento.*
    Barcelona: Herder, 1973.

Schultz, Anselm. "Formas fundamentales de la parenesis primi-
    tiva." In *Forma y próposito del Nuevo Testamento,* ed. Josef
    Schreiner. Barcelona: Herder, 1973.

*Shiva, Vandana. *Stolen Harvest: The Hijacking of the Global
    Food Supply.* Cambridge, Mass.: South End Press, 2000.
    #3463, $14.00.

Sider, Ronald J. *Rich Christians in an Age of Hunger: Moving from
    Affluence to Generosity.* Dallas: Word Books, 1997.

———. *Just Generosity: A New Vision for Overcoming Poverty in
    America.* Grand Rapids, Mich.: Baker Book House, 1999.

Sleeper, C. Freeman. *James.* Abingdon New Testament Commen-
    taries. Nashville: Abingdon Press, 1998.

Sobrino, Jon. *La oración de Jesús y del cristiano.* Mexico City:
    CRT, 1981.

Stegemann, Wolfgang. *The Gospel and the Poor.* Philadelphia:
    Fortress Press, 1984.

Tamez, Elsa. *The Bible of the Oppressed.* Maryknoll, N.Y.: Orbis
    Books, 1982.

Townsend, Michael J. *The Epistle of James.* Epworth Commen-
    taries. London: Epworth Press, 1994.

Vaage, Leif E., ed. and trans. *Subversive Scriptures: Revolutionary
    Readings of the Christian Bible in Latin America.* Valley Forge,
    Pa.: Trinity Press International, 1997.

Wall, Robert W. *Community of the Wise: The Letter of James.* New Testament in Context. Valley Forge, Pa.: Trinity Press International, 1997.

Wesley, John. "A Plain Account of Christian Perfection." In *John and Charles Wesley: Selected Prayers, Hymns, Journal Notes, Sermons, Letters and Treatises,* ed. Frank Whaling. Classics of Western Spirituality. New York: Paulist Press, 1981.

Wesley, John. "Of True Christian Faith." In *John Wesley,* ed. Albert C. Outler. New York: Oxford University Press, 1964.

Williams, George H. *Radical Reformation.* Philadelphia: Westminster, 1962; Span. trans.: *La reforma radical.* Mexico City: Fondo de Cultura Económica, 1983.

Study Guide

The Scandalous Message
of James

Pamela Sparr

Introduction

This guide is intended to assist those who will be leading or facilitating the spiritual growth study on *The Scandalous Message of James* based on the text by Elsa Tamez. While the primary participants in this study will be members of United Methodist Women in Schools of Christian Mission and in local units, this resource is designed so that the suggested study format can be adapted for use in local church mission or Bible study groups or other settings with other audiences. Before deciding on any plan of action, please read both the book and study guide in their entirety.

Opportunities This Study Presents

Rarely has it happened that the nationality of the author of the spiritual growth study matches the topic of a geographical mission study for United Methodist Women. Because Elsa Tamez is Mexican and brings a Latin American reading to the book of James, there may be wonderful opportunities for cross-pollination between this mission study and the one on Mexico, with economic justice issues as the link. Leaders for these two studies who will be working at the same location may want to discuss in advance the topics they will cover; perhaps some cooperative efforts might be useful and enjoyable. It may be helpful to have one class session held together, for members of one study group to offer a report or presentation to supplement the other, or for both groups to watch a common video, for example. Possible topics shared between the two studies include:

- poverty in Mexico
- Mexican Americans living in poverty
- the contemporary Zapatista movement
- the "preferential option for the poor" and Latin American liberation theology
- the political and economic history of the U.S.-Mexican relationship
- current and proposed free trade agreements with Mexico (North American Free Trade Agreement and the Free Trade Area of the Americas)
- U.S.-Mexican border issues and border ministries within The United Methodist Church

Resources for the mission study theme on Mexico available from the General Board of Global Ministries Service Center include: *Mexico: Labyrinth of Faith* adult text: English #3181; Spanish #3182, $7.50; *Amazin' Mexico* CD-ROM #3186, $6.00; and Map of Mexico #3187, $8.95.

Studying the New Testament Letter of James is politically timely. In 2002, the United States Congress will be reconsidering welfare policy, as the Clinton administration's path-breaking welfare reform legislation comes up for reauthorization. Once again, there will be national debate about a national policy on poverty and the appropriate role of federal and state governments. Poverty is a priority issue for the Women's Division and United Methodist Women as well as The United Methodist Church. It will be important for members of United Methodist Women—indeed, all Christians—to become informed and participate in shaping our new public policy. Welfare policy might be an excellent case study for wrestling with the meaning of the Letter of James for us today.

John Wesley stressed putting faith into action in everyday life. This Wesleyan tradition resonates with the message of the Letter of James. Advocacy on behalf of women and children, the dispossessed and oppressed around the world lies at the mission heart of the organization of United Methodist Women. This spiritual growth study offers United Methodist Women members an opportunity to dig deeper into their souls, to stretch and grow as Christians, and to understand the biblical basis for our collective mission in a deeper way.

Challenges to Leading This Study

As is often the case, this opportunity to reflect personally upon a strong biblical mandate for putting faith into action also presents study leaders with some challenges. If we are to do justice to both the text of James and that of Elsa Tamez, there is no way we can avoid some difficult theological and emotional material.

On the theological front, we are first confronted with the authorship of James. Who is James? Does the ambiguity around his identity really matter ultimately? Then we wade into deep water surrounding the Second Coming and concepts of universal salvation. For example, if God is compassionate and merciful, why should the rich dread judgment and have anything to fear in the end? What does it mean for the poor that they will participate in the New World and others will not? Does this mean that some are not really "saved"? Can people who are not materially poor be Christian?

In the text, we note that James and John Wesley agree that good Christians should not cause divisions among people and within communities. However, when James harshly disparages the rich and urges people to work mightily to undo injustices, as well as to be honest with themselves and others, can this be avoided, even if done with loving kindness? Don't Christians, including United Methodist Women, avoid tackling the justice issues precisely because they want to avoid hurting people's feelings? Because they do not want to cause division within church or community? Or, because of wealthy members' financial support of the church?

These are examples of some of the thorny questions that

the Tamez and James texts raised for me. Study leaders should list the questions that arise in their reading of the material and try to predict those that might emerge for the participants in their class sessions. While these questions can be discussed intellectually, leaders will need to be prepared for the emotional impact participants will experience as they engage in readings, discussions, and activities. Clearly, this is not emotionally neutral subject matter.

The texts challenge us to be honest about our economic class identity. What is our own economic status? Do we understand where we stand in the web of global economic interdependence and oppressive relationships? How do we live with this understanding? What does this mean for our definition and practice of Christianity? Discussing our personal financial circumstances openly and honestly is difficult for anyone in the United States, especially in a church or other religious setting. Many remain unaware that this silence or discomfort reflects class oppression at work. For many women, particularly those who are middle class or perhaps affluent, keeping silent may seem the polite thing to do—again without realizing that this is class oppression at work. First to reveal one's economic status and then to explore critically how one's economic status might affect personal religious beliefs may be a new and perhaps unsettling experience for some.

Study leaders will need to plan carefully in advance how they want to focus the discussion. How will you navigate a course that addresses difficult key issues thoughtfully? How will you structure a conversation that is honest and real and doesn't leave people feeling sunk in embarrassment or guilt or relieved by simplistic answers or rationalizations? For this study to be worthwhile, the leader must be willing to take emotional and intellectual risks in guiding the discussions, and in modeling the honesty and openness being asked of participants. Knowing your strengths and weaknesses as a facilitator will help you select those topics you feel capable of handling. Keep in mind that the point is not to avoid controversy or difficult feelings—in you or among participants. A "successful" class session is likely to involve some tears, some lingering doubts, some powerful debate and discussion. Each session of this study guide contains tips for activities and strategies for productive conversations on some of these difficult issues.

Preparing to Lead

1. Obtain the text for this study, *The Scandalous Message of James: Faith Without Works Is Dead* ($6.00) by Elsa Tamez well in advance from the General Board of Global Ministries Service Center (see full ordering information on p. 178).

2. Read the Letter of James several times, highlighting what you think are the important passages. Go to a public library or your church library and read several biblical translations of James to see how the language differs and if this significantly affects the meaning of any key passages. Begin with the Jerusalem Bible quoted in the Tamez text and contrast it with the New Revised Standard Version. See if you can borrow several versions to have by your side as you read the study book. You might want to have several different translations or editions of the Bible on hand for your class participants to use. Use the Internet at **www.biblegateway.com** to search key concepts such as "rich," "wealthy," "poor," etc. to identify key biblical passages about wealth and poverty or other themes you want to use with your class. These references will help you compare and contrast James's message with other books in the Bible.

3. Read the study book by Elsa Tamez several times, taking notes of the passages or sections you find particularly helpful or striking both intellectually and emotionally. Although this session guide contains text-related discussion questions, you may want to add or substitute your own. List discussion questions as you do your reading.

4. Read this study guide carefully before deciding on a

course of action. In fact, you might want to read James and
Tamez once, this study guide once, and then go back and
read James and Tamez again with the study guide suggestions
and questions in mind. Do some more investigation of possible focus issues and activities before finalizing your plans.
See step 6 below for more details.

5. Review the bibliography on pp. 81–86, Additional Resources on p. 169, and the contact information listed in
Appendix C on p. 154. Obtain as many books as you feel
able to read. In particular, two areas where you might want
to bolster your knowledge are Luther and his time, and
Roman Catholic social teaching, particularly as it applies to
the "preferential option for the poor" within liberation theology. The United Nations Development Program's *Human
Development Report 1999* provides an excellent summary of
global inequalities and poverty trends. It can be ordered from
bookstores. The Women's Division's UMOUN office, 777
UN Plaza, New York, NY 10017, may be able to obtain the
shorter summary version for you. Contact some of the groups
mentioned in Appendix C for more information on relevant
topics. Ask for materials you might use in your class, political
updates as background information, free handouts, etc.

6. Scan listed Web sites and make notes or print out Web
pages that you might want to use in your classes or have as
background. See especially the Women's Division Web site:

http://gbgm-umc.org/umw/james

Also see the John Wesley Web site, which contains text of
sermons on relevant topics such as perfection, riches, and integrity:

http://gbgm-umc.org/umw/wesley

7. If you are teaching in a Regional or Conference School
of Christian Mission or another setting where the geographical study will be offered simultaneously with yours, consider
contacting the study leaders to see whether any kind of collaboration among the classes on James and Mexico would
be productive.

8. You will find it very helpful to borrow or buy *The Book of Resolutions of The United Methodist Church, 2000* and *The Book of Discipline of The United Methodist Church, 2000* (available from Cokesbury: 1-800-672-1789; $14.00 each). In The *Book of Resolutions,* reread the Social Principles (pp. 37–64, especially "The Social Community" [¶162] and "The Economic Community" [¶163]). Become familiar with the resolutions related to Economic Justice. Also read "Our Theological Task" (¶104.4, pp. 74–86) in *The Book of Discipline.* Your understanding of United Methodist positions and principles will provide an essential foundation to your leadership of this study.

9. Be sure to review the Women's Division's policy statement on giving, *Mission: Responding to God's Grace* (#2581, 50¢ ea. + postage), as well as the policy statement *Ministries with Women and Ministries with Children and Youth: A Gift for the Whole Church* (#1892, 30¢ ea. + postage). Have a copy of each available for the participants in the class.

10. Provide copies of *Global Praise 1* (#2572, $6.95 + postage) and *Global Praise 2* (#2918, $8.95 + postage) songbooks and/or *The United Methodist Hymnal* if you select hymns from them for session opening and closing worship times. (Use the *Hymnal's* "Index of Topics and Categories," which begins on p. 934, to look for hymns other than those mentioned.) Provide other songbooks such as *The Faith We Sing* or copies of other music you select. See pp. 169 and 171.

11. Many recent Reading Program book selections relate to this study theme, including:

- *Faith in a Global Economy: A Primer for Christians* (#3118, $9.95)

- *Free the Children: A Young Man Fights against Child Labor* (#3120, $13.00)

- *Preaching Justice: Ethnic and Cultural Perspectives* (#3154, $14.95)

- *The Good Society: The Humane Agenda* (#3127, $13.00)

- *Urban Churches, Vital Signs: Beyond Charity Toward Justice* (#3171, $15.00)

Also see the bibliography on pp. 81–86. Check with the local public library for availability or order from the United Methodist General Board of Global Ministries Service Center, using the stock numbers.

12. Review recent editions of *Response* and *New World Outlook* magazines with themes relevant to this study. Some *Response* issues that may be helpful are: October 2000 (Indigenous Peoples); December 2000 (Being Rich and Being Faithful); February 2001 (World Trade); May 2002, #3199, $1.50 (Mexico); April 2002, #3198, $1.50 (Restorative Justice).

13. Think and pray about the people who will participate in this study. What do you know about the experiences, assumptions, expectations, and biases they might bring? Are theirs similar to or different from yours? Take all this into consideration when developing your goals for the study and as you select activities that will contribute toward meeting those goals. Spending time in prayer throughout the experience is important. Leading any study, especially one of such critical importance personally and socially, and therefore emotionally charged, is a serious responsibility. Seek God's help and presence.

14. Outline all sessions. Then develop details, including allotments of time for activities, worship, etc. for the first two sessions. After each session, you will want to review and amend the content of the next session as necessary and add details. Be flexible. Allow the group to pursue a particular issue or activity if it wishes to do so. Make a list in advance of all the supplies and handouts needed for the activities you are planning. It is better to be overprepared than not to have what you need. If you are not a singer or do not want to rely

on another class member to lead singing, add a tape or CD player to your list of equipment. *Global Praise,* for example, is available on CD. This will enable you to incorporate music into worship and other sections of the study.

Room Preparation

Prepare the meeting room. Arrive well ahead of time for each session, and particularly for the first. Some of the details of room preparation include:

Room Fundamentals

- Check the room for **space needs.** Is it large enough for the number of people you anticipate with room for movement? Is it amenable to small and large group work?

- Are there enough **chairs?** What kind of **tables** do you want to use for display or activities?

- Check the **lighting** to ensure sufficient brightness and ability to control glare from windows or lights.

- Check the **sound quality.** Does the room echo or are there loud noises in the vicinity that might make hearing difficult?

- Check the **policy about displaying items** on walls or find an alternative way of decorating the space and posting information.

- Check for the **availability of a wall writing board or portable easel for newsprint** to use for writing agendas and assignments and taking notes during group discussions. If possible, avoid dry erase boards that create dust and dry erase or permanent magic markers. Their dust and fumes are unhealthy and cause allergic reactions in some people.

- Check that the **room temperature** is comfortable and that you know how to adjust it.

- Know the location of the nearest **rest rooms** and build comfort breaks into your teaching plans.

Arrangement of Chairs

A circle, semicircle, or concentric circles usually works best to convey openness and community and to encourage active participation. Chairs with attached writing surfaces will enable participants to take notes and balance books more easily. If the group is small, you may want to work around tables. However, be sure to allow enough open space for movement and activities. Ideally, you will want to vary large and small group activities. Moveable chairs and tables help facilitate good group process. Some activities work best with no tables or other obstructions between people. The least desirable setting is a room with immovable seats with everyone facing forward, such as an auditorium or traditional sanctuary. If you are assigned to an auditorium or sanctuary, use a cordless microphone or one with a long cord to allow people to share and hear comments. If your microphone is stationary, repeat questions and comments into the microphone so all can hear them and follow the dialogue.

Room Decoration

People work best in a room that feels inviting and stimulating (but not overly stimulating). Judiciously displaying pictures, photos, charts and graphs, catchy or inspiring phrases, flowers, objects related to the discussion all add to the environment. Nonverbal, sensory additions to the décor and activities help balance the verbal and rational dimensions of the learning experience. In order to avoid sensory overload and to keep the class interested over time, consider adding some new decorations at each session rather than displaying everything for the entire time.

A Word about This Study Guide

Basic Assumptions

This study guide makes some assumptions:

1. All participants will have read the assigned chapters from the basic text by Elsa Tamez and the Letter of James prior to each session. Participants will bring both their Bibles and the Tamez text to each session.

2. The study is designed for four two-hour sessions but can be adapted for other formats.

3. A variety of teaching and learning methods ensures a more effective study. Each session outline suggests a variety of activities that utilize different learning methods for you to choose from. Regardless of the activities you plan for sessions, be sure that active group participation occurs and that participants are encouraged to do some personal reflection before each class.

Use of Themes

The suggested themes for each session parallel the main topic headings in *The Scandalous Message of James*. Elsa Tamez offers *praxis* as a way of putting faith into action. However she does not discuss the practicalities of how one might do this in everyday life. To give participants some handles, the learning activities are designed to illustrate a process for praxis as a continuous spiral of experience, action, and reflection—the "spiral of praxis." See p. 143.

Worship

Facilitators may ask class volunteers to plan opening and closing worship meditations as a way of sharing leadership. Encourage those in charge to consider developing a common theme to unify all the worship times throughout the duration of the study. Bread might be a unifying theme. Bread is often used as a metaphor for material possessions, money, the things we need for basic sustenance. Who has it and who does not is a central issue for the writer of James. Bread is

Some General Principles
of Adult Education

These are subtle foundations for "praxis."

1. The process is participatory. We build on everyone's experience and knowledge. This is not the typical formal education style in which an "expert" exclusively feeds information to people, assuming that participants come with nothing to offer. Everyone teaches, everyone learns.

2. We develop our analysis and strategies through group process. We exist in community. We start from our own life experience.

3. An atmosphere of trust and respect for each person's experience and knowledge is critically important to the process.

4. The educational process is designed to be empowering, not disempowering.

5. People learn in many different ways—through verbal and visual means, through action and reading, through personal journaling, thought and study, etc. Education works best when it recognizes and uses a variety of approaches.

6. We model teamwork and cooperation in our education, not competition and individualism.

also a powerful Christian symbol. One possibility in planning the opening or closing meditations for each day is to use variations on the Lord's Prayer and the theme of "our daily bread."

Another possible worship theme is "be doers of the word and not hearers only." So much of worship traditionally involves hearing, speaking, and referring to text (whether the Bible, a hymnal, the bulletin for the service, etc.). One approach would be to avoid using anything printed for worship

7. The process and its results are based on the needs of the group, not on the facilitator's needs.

8. It must be fun! (This does not mean that the process is not serious or difficult at times.)

9. Education works best when it is multidimensional, reaching people at the intellectual, sensory, emotional, physical, and spiritual levels.

10. The purpose of the educational experience is to lead to action for social change.

11. Because of the way many of us have been raised and the signals and incentives our society gives to women, we have some special needs when it comes to justice-oriented, faith-based educational processes. Many women have not had the opportunity to think big about their own lives or how the world might be different. We need to be encouraged to do so. Many also have not had the chance to develop and sharpen their critical thinking skills. We need to be challenged to do so. Rare is the opportunity for women to have the time and safe environment to uncover their deepest longings, their frustrations, fears, anger, and hurts related to their economic security. If we are to build a just world for all, women's feelings, dreams, and best thinking about the economy must be nurtured.

and thereby possibly enhancing the experience by freeing up hands, eyes, ears, and hearts in a new way. How might worship be created as a way of acting out being "doers of the word"?

Ground Rules for Class Participation

Regardless of how well the participants know each other, consider establishing ground rules in the first session. Basic rules help create a greater sense of safety in the group and promote good dialogue. These ground rules can be developed by the class or the facilitator can suggest them and ask for comment and agreement by the class. Possible items for the list include:

- honoring the confidentiality of statements made in class

- sharing only to the level of comfort

- raising all questions; there is no such thing as a "dumb question"

- speaking no more than once (or twice) before everyone has had a chance to speak at least once

- speaking in "I" statements rather than in generalizations or telling someone else's story

- not interrupting

- paying attention to gender and race to ensure everyone is heard. While this is not outlined in detail for the first session, it is mentioned in the list of goals

Another important building block is participants' expectations for the study. Discussing these early on will help the facilitator to fine-tune the curriculum and to address those expectations unlikely to be met. This also sends a signal to participants to expect to be active participants (not just passive recipients) in shaping an effective learning experience. Again, note this is mentioned as a goal for Session 1 but not elaborated. As with handling introductions and ground rules, facilitators will devise a process for discussing expectations with which they feel comfortable.

Sample Discussion Questions for the Letter of James and *The Scandalous Message of James*

For the Letter of James

Chapter 1

- What kinds of communities would have heard or read this message?
- What were their trials?
- How might different communities respond to James's message in different ways?
- Why was the letter written to these communities?
- Why did the writer think actions based on faith were key?
- What kinds of actions did he emphasize?

Chapter 2

- What is the "law of freedom"?
- To whom does James show partiality? For the poor?
- Does that partiality have any parallels today in The United Methodist Church or United Methodist Women?

Chapter 3

- Why does James focus on speech as being so dangerous? Do you agree?
- What characteristics of wisdom does he think are important?

Chapter 4

- James talks about the difference between being a friend of the world vs. a friend of God. Why was this an issue in his day?
- What are examples of these two postures today?
- Where do you see this tension cropping up in your life?

- Given James's critique of people planning on making money for the future, how do you think he would react to IRAs, 401(k)s, unemployment insurance, social security, people investing in stock options and futures?

Chapter 5

- What is the problem with being rich in James's eyes? Do you agree?
- Why do you think James focuses his critique on the rich?
- What kind of patience is he after?
- Why is swearing an oath so important for James? Does this have any relevance to your life?
- What can and should the Christian community do for each other and do together?

For **The Scandalous Message of James**
Chapter 1

- Why was the James text so controversial as the biblical canon was formed?
- What do we know about the author of this book of the Bible?
- Does it matter who the author was?

Chapter 2

- Who was oppressed in James's time?
- What does being oppressed mean?
- The mission of United Methodist Women is to work with the oppressed and challenge oppressors. Who are they today?
- Who were they for James?
- How do they behave?
- How should we relate to oppressors? To the oppressed?

- Can the wealthy belong to the Christian community?
- Where should the oppressed worship? Where do they today?

Chapter 3

- What kinds of hope are there?
- Why should we have hope?
- What do we do with our hope?
- What does hope look like?
- What will the End Time look like?
- Where does suffering come from?
- What does it mean if God has favorites?
- What should rich Christians do?
- What should poor Christians do?
- Can we reconcile James's commands not to be judgmental and to watch our speech with his other command to work for justice on behalf of the poor? If so, how?

Chapter 4

- What is praxis? How do we do it?
- What does "militant patience" mean?
- What does integrity mean for James? How do we demonstrate it?
- Elsa Tamez makes the point that the church acting out of a desire for self-preservation errs too much on the side of worldly conformity—incorporating the society's values and practices. Do you see examples of this now? If so, where?
- What does the "perfect law of freedom" mean? What is its relationship to the "law of service"?
- What does James say about prayer?

Chapter 5

This is a short, very helpful recap of key points made in previous chapters.

Appendix

- What were John Wesley's thoughts on James?
- What did Wesley mean by "Christian perfection" or "sanctification"?
- How does Wesley view salvation? How do you?

Introducing
the Study of James

Goals for the Session

1. **To get to know each other.** Take some time for introductions. Ask each person about her hopes and expectations for the class.

2. **To build community, including establishing ground rules for the class.** Accomplish this through the opening worship, introductions, and a conversation about how you will operate as a group together, among other things.

3. **To agree on goals for the study—establishing purpose and focus.** Discuss how you had planned to structure the class and how it fits with participants' expectations. Fine-tune your agenda together, if necessary.

4. **To understand the context of James.** This is accomplished through one or more learning activities. Suggestions appear below.

Readings Done in Advance by Participants

- Letter of James (*ideal, but not necessary*)

- Study text: Chapter 1 (*ideal, but not necessary*)

Opening Worship

Scripture: James 1:22–25

Hymn

Choose one on the theme "be doers of the word and not just hearers." Possibilities include:

"Here I Am, Lord" (#593, *The United Methodist Hymnal*)

"Guide My Feet" (#68, *Global Praise 1*)

"What Does the Lord Require of You" (#174, *The Faith We Sing*)

"The Summons" (#130, *The Faith We Sing*)

Prayer

Holy One, we are here, eager to discern your will for us, and to grow in our faith. Open our minds so that we can explore new ideas and dare to dream new dreams. Open our ears to drink in the experience, wisdom, and feelings of others. Open our hearts so that we can be moved in unexpected, fresh ways. Dear God, we realize it is very easy to slip into complacency and just coast along. So we ask you to use the opportunity of this class to both heal our wounds and trouble our hearts where we have become too comfortable. Help us to be powerful doers of your word and not just hearers only. Amen.

Primary Activities

1. Survey of the Text and Pantomime

Divide the class into five small groups. Assign to each group a chapter of the Letter of James to read. Encourage use of different biblical translations. Ask them to pick out key "proverbs" or commonly known sayings in that chapter and write them on newsprint banners. Ask each group to devise a pantomime for one phrase and then present it for the larger group to guess what it is. Post the banners in the room for the entire course of the study. Conclude by referencing other types of wise sayings in Scripture with similar messages such as proverbs, parables, and the Beatitudes.

2. *Mock Debate/Hypothetical Conversations*

Stage a mock debate among Martin Luther, "James," and John Wesley regarding whether or not the text of James should be included in the biblical canon. Break the group into three small teams: a Luther team, a James team, and a Wesley team. Each team will select one person to represent the point of view in the debate. The facilitator may want to provide each team with a few basic arguments to help it get started. If a debater gets tired or stuck, invite someone else from the team to step in. Ask a person from each team to list the pro's and con's for its point of view as the debate progresses. Take a few minutes after the debate to debrief the comments and arguments. An alternative version is to put James and Paul, Mary and Martha, and Esther together to talk about their perspective on the relative merits of faith and works. The facilitator should provide a quote for each character to help him or her get started.

3. *Time Travel Role Play*

Explain that Martin Luther, "James," John Wesley, and a UMW member will all be contestants in an episode of *Survivor* located in the Mall of America in Minnesota. (This is the largest mall in the United States, if not the world.) Have other members of the class be shop owners, store clerks, and customers who interact with the four and set up challenges for them. What challenges should the contestants face to bring out the key themes in James? How would they handle them? How would the contestants talk or act towards each other (in a historically appropriate way for their own time)? How would you determine who the "winner" is? The point of this exercise lies as much in the preparatory planning and discussion phase and any debriefing you choose to do as in the actual enacting of the *Survivor* episode. To prepare, make sure you or someone who can help you is familiar with the TV show *Survivor.* This might be a good way to involve younger people.

4. Small Group Discussions

Break the class into three small groups. Have each group read chapter 1 of James. All the small groups should read the chapter looking for key messages and themes that appear. Group 1 should then discuss which of these key messages or themes would be controversial or "scandalous" for James's time. Who would find them so? Why? Group 2 should evaluate the themes from the perspective of what would be controversial for Luther reading James. (It might be helpful for the facilitator to give a very brief background on the theological and historical context of late fifteenth-century and early sixteenth-century Europe.) Group 3 should evaluate the themes from the perspective of today. What is "scandalous" or "controversial" for mainstream people living in the United States today? Why? Small groups report their findings and ideas back to the large group.

– OR –

Have five small groups, each reading one chapter of James and answering the question from the perspectives of James, Luther, and contemporary Christians.

5. Bible Search: Making Connections

One of the ways participants might evaluate Luther's argument that the Letter of James does not belong in the Bible is to ask participants to discover similar messages in James and other books of the Bible such as the Prophets, Psalms, and the Gospels. Depending on the biblical literacy of the group, the facilitator might want to provide some hints to participants to get them going. One such example is Mary's "Magnificat" in Luke 1:46–55 (**http://www.biblegateway.com** is an excellent on-line resource for discovering where similar phrases and concepts appear in the Bible). Divide the class into five smaller groups. Assign each group a chapter of

James. Give each group about 20 minutes to identify similar concepts in other parts of the Bible. Reconvene into a large group for reporting back and synthesizing findings.

Suggested Assignments for Special Reports and Activities

Faith in Action Research Groups

Offer the class a list of economic justice topics that relate to the themes in James and have an important presence of the faith community in the campaign or particular struggle for justice. Some possible issues include:

- Jobs with Justice—living wage campaigns in the U.S.
- Welfare Reauthorization/Reform and poor people's organizing in the U.S.
- the farmworker movement in the U.S.
- The Zapatista movement and the struggle for indigenous people's rights in Mexico
- The global Jubilee movement for debt cancellation
- Free trade/fair trade and the World Trade Organization.

Ask class members to select a topic group. Not all issues need be covered. Not all groups need the same number of people in each. Offer each group resources on the topic, including Web sites, printed materials, books, and magazines. (See the bibliography, p. 81; Appendix C, p. 154; and Additional Resources, pp. 169–172.) Ask them to prepare a presentation or activity for the last day of class session. Give each group a minimum of 10–15 minutes to share what they have learned depending on the number of groups and your plans for the last session.

Suggest some focus questions. (If not all the participants have this study guide, consider putting the focus questions on a handout or newsprint sheets for each group's use.)

- What are the justice issues involved?

- Where and in what ways have people of faith gotten involved with these issues or struggle?

- What current challenges and opportunities do these issues pose for the faith community?

- What did you find to be inspiring in your research?

- What did you learn that was new, and what new insights did you get about putting your faith into action?

As facilitator, check ahead of time to see if there are groups or campaigns locally involved in one or more of these issues. If so, consider a special meeting or field trip to learn about the issue firsthand. Or you might see how your class could perform some service or action in solidarity with the local group or campaign.

Create a Personal Timeline

Invite members of the class to use some of the key themes in James to reflect on their life's path and where they are spiritually at this moment. Possible themes include: faith and action, money and poverty, the role of oppression, justice and hope in their lives. Each day provide them with a set of reflection questions (see Appendix B, p. 150). Invite participants to reflect on the questions, make some notes, and visually chart highlights on a personal timeline outside of the class. Creating this timeline privately encourages members to wrestle with the meaning of the study material in a more detailed and honest way, knowing they will not be asked to share anything unless they choose to do so. The purpose of this exercise is to enable participants to examine what may be fragmented or compartmentalized parts of themselves so that they may be able to assess their beliefs and actions with fresh eyes; to see new connections between their past experiences and who they are today; and to obtain insights about future directions for their lives. Encourage participants not to feel overwhelmed by the questions. Try a few in class and remind them that they can always continue this reflection process later at home if they wish.

It would be helpful to provide each class member with blank timeline paper that is 8 ½″ x 14″ or 11″ x 17″. Encourage people to draw their timeline horizontally using the widest dimension of the paper. They should mark their beginning point by giving the day they were born and the location.

Suggest that the participants think about the day's questions and jot some notes down to answer them. Encourage them to try to visualize key events related to the issues raised by the questions. Visualization may help them remember details, including feelings, thoughts, and people involved. Once they have recalled important memories and answered the questions, they can begin to represent them graphically on their timeline with key words, pictures, and symbols related to dates or time periods they write on the line. The spacing does not have to be mathematically proportional (e.g., one inch equals five years), but events or trends should be in chronological order going from left to right. The right edge of the page should represent the present moment. (They may want to put more than one piece of paper together to have a longer timeline and have more space for noting events, trends, etc.)

Participants might want to chart their answers to each day's questions in different colors. This might help them make new connections and insights when they finish their chart. Another option is to draw parallel timelines—one for each set of questions on the same paper, with them appearing on top of each other like layers in a layer cake. Encourage flexibility of style—whatever works to promote reflection and analysis.

Tip: At each session, as facilitator you may want to model drawing a few answers to the assigned reflection questions on your own timeline. This will help people understand how to get started on their homework assignment.

Suggested Assignments

1. Read chapter 1 (if not already read) and chapter 2 in the study text, and all of the Letter of James in preparation for the next session.

2. Read the questions for Step #1, "Your Economic History," for the timeline exercise (p. 150).

Closing Worship

Sing a hymn such as:

"Sois la Semilla" "You Are the Seed" (#583, *The United Methodist Hymnal*)

"God of Grace and God of Glory" (#577, *The United Methodist Hymnal*)

"Move Me" (#471, *The United Methodist Hymnal*)

One of those listed for the Opening Worship

Prayer

Say the traditional form of the Lord's Prayer in unison.

– Session 2 –

Exploring the Nature of Oppression in the Letter's and Our Times

Goals for the Session

1. To understand the Letter of James regarding wealth, poverty, and oppression.

2. To examine economic and political life when the Letter was written, and to understand James's relevance for today by contrasting its context with life today.

3. To identify our own socioeconomic position, considering what it might mean for our interpretation of James and what God calls us to do.

Opening Worship

Scripture: James 5:1–6

Meditation: Rich Woman, Poor Woman

This meditation should be read by two women, perhaps standing back to back—facing away from each other. Alternatively, it could be read responsively with the group split into two. This reflection was written by a working-class Chilean woman in 1973, shortly after the military coup that overthrew Chile's democratically elected Socialist president, Salvador Allende. A U.S. missionary translated the work and brought it with her when she was forced to leave Chile.

I am a woman.
I AM A WOMAN.

I am a woman whose man wore silk suits, who constantly watched his weight.
I AM A WOMAN WHOSE MAN WORE TATTERED CLOTHING, WHOSE HEART WAS CONSTANTLY STRANGLED BY HUNGER.

I am a woman who watched two babies grow into beautiful children.
I AM A WOMAN WHO WATCHED TWO BABIES DIE BECAUSE THERE WAS NO MILK.

I am a woman who watched twins grow into popular college students with summers abroad.
I AM A WOMAN WHO WATCHED THREE CHILDREN GROW, BUT WITH BELLIES STRETCHED FROM NO FOOD.

But then there was a man,
BUT THEN THERE WAS A MAN.

And he talked about the peasants getting richer by my family getting poorer.
AND HE TOLD ME OF DAYS THAT WOULD BE BETTER AND HE MADE THE DAYS BETTER.

We had to eat rice.
WE HAD RICE.

We had to eat beans!
WE HAD BEANS.

My children were no longer given summer visas to Europe.
MY CHILDREN NO LONGER CRIED THEMSELVES TO SLEEP.

And I felt like a peasant.
AND I FELT LIKE A WOMAN.

A peasant with a dull, hard, unexciting life.
LIKE A WOMAN WITH A LIFE THAT SOMETIMES ALLOWED A SONG.

And I saw a man.
AND I SAW A MAN.

And together we began to plot with the hope of the return to freedom.
I SAW HIS HEART BEGAN TO BEAT WITH HOPE OF FREEDOM, AT LAST.

Someday, the return to freedom.
SOME DAY, FREEDOM.

And then,
BUT THEN,

One day,
ONE DAY,

There were planes overhead and guns firing close by.
THERE WERE PLANES OVERHEAD AND GUNS FIRING IN THE DISTANCE.

I gathered my children and went home.
I GATHERED MY CHILDREN AND RAN.

And the guns moved further and further away.
BUT THE GUNS MOVED CLOSER AND CLOSER.

And then they announced that freedom had been restored!
AND THEN, THEY CAME, YOUNG BOYS REALLY . . .

They came into my home along with my man.
THEY CAME AND FOUND MY MAN.

Those men whose money was almost gone.
THEY FOUND ALL OF THE MEN WHOSE LIVES WERE ALMOST THEIR OWN.

And we all had drinks to celebrate.
AND THEY SHOT THEM ALL.

The most wonderful martinis.
THEY SHOT MY MAN.

And then they asked us to dance.
AND THEN THEY CAME FOR US.

Me.
FOR ME, THE WOMAN.

And my sisters.
FOR MY SISTERS.

And then they took us.
THEN TOOK US.

They took us to dinner at a small, private club.
THEY STRIPPED FROM US THE DIGNITY WE HAD GAINED.

And they treated us to beef.
AND THEN THEY RAPED US.

It was one course after another.
ONE AFTER THE OTHER THEY CAME AT US.

We nearly burst we were so full.
LUNGING, PLUNGING . . . SISTERS BLEEDING. SISTERS DYING.

It was magnificent to be free again!
IT WAS HARDLY A RELIEF TO HAVE SURVIVED.

And then we gathered the children together.
AND THEN, THEY TOOK OUR CHILDREN.

And he gave them some good wine.
AND THEN THEY TOOK THEIR SCISSORS.

And then we gave them a party.
AND THEY TOOK THE HANDS OF OUR CHILDREN. . . .

The beans have almost disappeared now.
THE BEANS HAVE DISAPPEARED.

The rice: I've replaced it with chicken or steak.
THE RICE, I CANNOT FIND IT.

And the parties continue, night after night to make up for all the time wasted.

AND MY SILENT TEARS ARE JOINED ONCE MORE
BY THE MIDNIGHT CRIES OF MY CHILDREN.

And I feel like a woman again.

THEY SAY, I AM A WOMAN.

Silent Meditation/Reflection

Hymn

"Cuando El Pobre" "When the Poor Ones" (#434, *The United Methodist Hymnal*)

"Break with the Hungry Your Own Bread" (#10, *Global Praise 1*)

"For Sake of Life" (#25, *Global Praise 1*)

Primary Activities

1. The "Good Times Café"

The "Good Times Café" is a participatory exercise designed for participants to locate themselves in the U.S. and global economic contexts.

Props: signs that say "Good Times Café" prominently displayed; at least one table set up with a tablecloth, food and beverages; cups, plates, serving utensils. The room set-up can be modified. Participants can all gather around one central table to experience the role play, or the facilitator can set up enough tables for five or six people per table to enact the role play in small groups. The point is to use a sample of food and beverage to demonstrate relative proportions of income of people both in the United States and globally. This works best with food and beverages that can be easily divided or measured out in order to handle the fractions. To illustrate this, a pie will be used for Round 1 and quart bottles of sparkling apple juice for Round 2.

Round 1: Income Distribution in the United States

Source of statistics:

U.S. Census Bureau for individuals over fifteen years old in 1999. See **http://www.census.gov/hhes/income** *for updated statistics.*

Ask the group to count off in fives to form small groups. Each person represents about 20 percent of the U.S. population fifteen years or older, or about 40 million people. In each group, person #1 represents the wealthiest 20 percent; #2, the second wealthiest 20 percent; etc. Person #5 represents the lowest income earners. The leader should emphasize that these statistics are for *income,* not wealth. Wealth is even more skewed in the United States than income. Updated statistics on wealth are harder to obtain than income.

Note: Income includes wages, salaries, pensions, royalties, interest and dividend earnings, government programs like Social Security.

Ask the group the following questions:

  a. If there were complete equality in people's incomes in the United States, how would the pie be divided among the five people? (Answer: everyone would have the same size slice.)

  b. How do you think the pie will be divided now? (Ask the group to brainstorm guesses.)

As leader, you will serve the pie according to current income distribution. First, cut it into equal quarters.

  To #5's (the bottom group), give a few crumbs from one of the quarter sections.

  To #4's (next-to-bottom group), give about one-third of the quarter section you just took the crumbs from.

  To #3's (middle group), give the rest of that quarter section.

To #4's (upper middle), give a full quarter.

To #5 (upper), give half the pie or two one-quarter sections.

Ask the group:

a. Based on your number in the group, how did you feel?

b. Were you surprised by the results? In what ways? Why?

c. Think back to your income tax forms for 1999. What was your income before deductions and credits? What is your actual place (or number) around the table? (*Note that participants may be very uneasy about discussing their economic circumstances openly. You might give each person a handout with income statistics on it and ask them to locate themselves visually in the chart.*)

d. Are you surprised by what you have learned?

At this point, the facilitator might want to show the actual Census Bureau statistics:

Individual Income—1999	Bottom 20%	2d 20%	3d 20%	4th 20%	5th 20%
Percentage of total income earned in 1999 earned by this group.	3.6%	9%	15%	23%	49.4%
Mean (average) income for a person in this group	$9,940	$24,436	$40,879	$63,555	$135,401

Another way to help people locate themselves is to look at the actual income ranges for roughly equal segments of the population. The unequal distribution is even more evident because the mean income figures listed above obscure wide differences. (*See the following table.*)

1999 Income of Persons— 15 years and older	Bottom 20%	2d 20%	3d 20%	4th 20%	5th 20%
Actual number of persons in this segment	40,523,000	34,916,000	37,234,000	37,425,000	45,538,000
Income range for people in this segment	Negative income to $7,499	$7,500– $14,999	$15,000– $24,999	$25,000– $39,999	$40,000 and up... *

Note: This category includes 6.5 million people who earned $100,000 or more.

Round 2: Global Incomes

If you are using a beverage for this round, it helps to use a glass liquid measuring cup to help determine serving sizes. In this round, the focus is the global income picture for 1998 using statistics from the UN Development Program's *Human Development Report 2000*.

There are roughly 6 billion people in the world. One-third live in two countries: 1.3 billion in China and almost 1 billion in India. The UN categorizes forty-six nations as "high human development." In this group the United States ranks no. 3, behind Canada and Norway. Slightly more than 1 billion people live in these countries enjoying a per capita income of $21,799. The UN labels ninety-three countries as "medium human development" (e.g., Costa Rica, the Philippines, Mexico, China, Egypt, India, Kenya, Zimbabwe). There are more than 4 billion people in this group, with a per capita income average of $3,458. (Note: China's per capita is $3,105 and India's is $2,077). In the "low human development group" there are thirty-seven nations (e.g., Haiti, Nigeria, Bangladesh, Nepal, Senegal, Yemen) with about 700 million people living on an average per capita income of $994.

Instruct people to count off in sixes. Identify each group as follows: #1, the wealthiest billion in the world; #2, the second wealthiest billion, and so on with #6 as the poorest billion people.

Before you do the exercise, ask everyone these questions:

1. What is your guess as to how the average income of a person in the United States compares with those in "medium" development nations like China or Mexico?

2. What is your guess as to how the average income of a person in the United States compares with someone in Haiti or Bangladesh?

Give each person in groups #1 through #6 the following amounts of beverage:

> Group #6: slightly less than 1 ounce of beverage (low human development nations)
>
> #5: 2 ounces of beverage (represents people of India)
>
> #4: 3 ounces of beverage (represents people of China)
>
> #3: 3 ½ ounces of beverage (other medium human development nations)
>
> #2: 3 ½ ounces of beverage (other medium human development nations)
>
> #1: 22 ounces of beverage (high human development nations)

In debriefing the second round, you as facilitator may want to remind people how averages such as per capita income obscure inequalities. Ask them to think about what they have just discussed regarding the United States. Similarly, global income disparities are even more grotesque than this simulation portrays.

Share these disturbing facts from the *1999 Human Development Report* (hand out a sheet to class members or write this list on newsprint for all to see):

- Nearly 1.3 billion people live on less than $1 a day.
- Close to 1 billion cannot meet their basic consumption requirements.

- An estimated 70 percent of the world's poor are females, who are also two-thirds of the world's illiterate people.

- The wealthiest 20 percent of the world's population live in countries that control and enjoy 86 percent of the world's goods and services, or Gross Domestic Product (GDP). The poorest 20 percent live in nations that control and enjoy 1 percent of global GDP.

- The assets of the three richest people in the world are more than the value of the goods and services produced in the poorest thirty-five countries in one year.

- The assets of the two hundred richest people in the world are more than the combined income of 41 percent of the world's people (2.5 billion). If these people donated 1 percent of their wealth annually, they could pay for the cost of primary education for all children around the world.

Discuss why and how this situation has come to exist. Some people may not feel much personal guilt, while others may be angry and overwhelmed by it.

- How can we be aware of the institutions, policies, and processes that create inequalities and poverty and maintain or exacerbate them?

- Do we understand (as U.S. residents) how we participate personally and collectively in structures or systems of sinfulness?

- In what ways are we oppressors or do we benefit from economic oppression?

- In what ways do we lose or get hurt by economic oppression?

- How do we use our power and position *collectively* to make a difference? (*Allow 15 minutes for discussion.*)

2. *Group Exercise: One Step Forward, Two Steps Back*

This exercise enables people to look at their race, class, and gender privileges. People often find it more comfortable to talk about oppression rather than privilege. This exercise provides a concrete and simple way to enter that discussion. It begins with everyone standing in a line. They each take a step forward or back, depending on how they personally answer questions put to the group. For a list of questions and instructions see the Web sites at

http: //www.diversitywork.org or
http: //www.toolsforchange/workshop_descriptions

Facilitators may want to underscore certain points such as:

- Do the people who have stepped forward look back?

- Where do the people in the middle look?

- Which group has the best view of the entire room? (people in back).

If people do not want to respond to a particular question, they do not have to move physically. Good questions for the facilitator to raise are: what kind of society would it take, and how could it be created, for people to feel safe to share?

3. *Sculpting Oppression*

The famous Russian writer and moralist Leo Tolstoy wrote a short story about a wealthy landlord who rides about on the back of a peasant. The landlord tries to do everything he can for the peasant—doesn't ask him to walk too quickly; points out from his higher vantage point the mud puddles and hazards looming along the way; makes sure he stops to eat and take breaks. The landlord, however, never realizes that the best thing he can do for the peasant is to get off his back! In what symbolic ways do we sit or stand on other people's shoulders without realizing it?

Step 1

Ask the group to brainstorm some of the people who are often invisible to us, but whose time, energy, talents, and natural resources go into making our lives comfortable, our needs and wants "affordable." Be sure to probe the economic, racial/ethnic, gender, geographic, and generational identity of people. Put some of the ideas on newsprint.

Step 2

Ask for a group of four to six volunteers to come to the center of the room. Invite them *in silence* to make a sculpture using their bodies and anything else in the room to depict some of the ways we sit or stand on others' shoulders.

Step 3

When this group is ready, invite the class to react, perhaps suggesting other versions of the oppression. (Volunteers can rearrange the sculpture!)

Step 4

Ask for another group of three volunteers to rearrange the sculpture to show how some people might offer charity to those suffering from oppression. Then ask them to show how the oppression might be dismantled and what a more just arrangement might look like. Again, this should be done in silence.

Step 5

Invite people to break into small groups or pairs. Ask them to answer these questions: In what ways have we created a comfortable, safe world for ourselves and those we live with? What do we take for granted in our lives (making no judgment upon it)? What reasons or rationalizations do we use to tell ourselves it is okay to be living the life we do? What are some of our fears about our life? What is the worst thing that could happen to us if we got out of our comfort zone?

What would getting out of our comfort zone require—if we were to get off the back of those who are oppressed?

4. Timeline

Carefully tape a long sheet of newsprint or shelf-liner paper to the wall horizontally. Ask the group to help construct a collective economic timeline. Put on the timeline key features of the economic situation in the time and context of James, of John Wesley, and of ourselves. Identify who was rich, who was poor, and who was in between.

- Were there slaves? Who were they?
- What was the economy like—subsistence, agricultural, nomadic, export-oriented, industrial?
- What was the culture of wealth like?
- What was the relationship between the economic elite and the religious elite?

This activity can be done as a large group with the facilitator asking the questions and charting the answers. Or three smaller groups could work on the three historical periods and report back to the entire group, charting the results. Having done this exercise and their personal timeline the night before (see p. 112), class members are ready to reflect on their insights regarding how James defines rich and poor, how they read James, and whether wealthy people can be part of the Christian community. See pp. 171–172 and Appendix C, p. 154 for Web resources to provide historical context information related to James and Wesley's time. Encyclopedia entries for "British Industrial Revolution" and "colonialism" can also provide background on economic conditions related to Wesley's time. Consider providing some written materials to participants to facilitate this exercise.

5. Newspapers—Rewriting James

Before the class session, purchase or borrow three to five newspapers from different parts of the United States or the world. Break into small groups depending on the number of newspapers you have to work with. Provide each small group with a newspaper and ask them to find a few striking current examples of economic injustice in the news. Ask them to pay attention to the wording of the articles and any particular point of view. Assign each group a relevant section of the Letter of James. Challenge them to paraphrase their section from James using current examples from their newspaper instead of the examples in the biblical text. Each group will need about 20–30 minutes to do its work. Ask each small group to read what it wrote to the large group during a report-back session. After each group reads its new paraphrase of James, ask all participants how they feel.

- Are they offended?
- Do they find this paraphrase more or less credible than the biblical version?
- Do they have any new insights into James or what it means to be a Christian as a result?
- Who might find this rewritten version of James scandalous or threatening?
- How might they react?
- What would happen if this new paraphrase were read during a worship service in participants' churches?

Suggested Assignments

1. Read chapter 3 and the Appendix of the study text, and the entire letter of James.

2. Read Step #2 for the personal timeline related to faith journeys (p. 151).

3. Read "The Service of the Poor and Spiritual Growth" by Albert Nolan, O.P., in *National Journal of the Chicago Religious Task Force on Central America* 2 (June 1991): "The Dilemma of the '90s: Economic Injustice,

Hunger and Hope in Latin America," pp. 50–53. See the summary in Activity 4 on pp. 141–43 ("Drama: The Service of the Poor and Stages of Spiritual Growth"); the text of the article appears on line at

http: //www.bfpubs.demon.co.uk/service.htm

4. An Experiment with Silence gives people the opportunity to think more about what James says about the tongue and speech and what it means to be powerless or without voice. Give everyone a sticky name tag (with backing still on) that says: "I have taken a vow of silence. Please don't expect me to speak." Ask people to take a vow of silence that will be observed some time before the last session. Silent time may be structured in a number of ways, for example, a particular time segment, such as three two-hour segments to be determined individually; or full participation during a certain meal time. Ask people to notice: how they felt; how people interacted with them; what opportunities they missed; what opportunities emerged as a result of being silent; what was hard; what they learned. Invite them to jot down notes for use in a discussion during the last session.

Closing Meditation

"Farm Worker Prayer" by Cesar Chavez (1927–93)

Show me the suffering of the most miserable;
so I will know my people's plight.

Free me to pray for others;
for you are present in every person.

Help me take responsibility for my own life;
so I can be free at last.

Grant me courage to serve others;
for in service there is true life.

Give me honesty and patience;
so that I can work with other workers.

Bring forth song and celebration;
so that the Spirit will be alive among us.

Let the Spirit flourish and grow;
so that we will never tire of the struggle.

Let us remember those who have died for justice;
for they have given us life.

Help us love even those who hate us;
so we can change the world.

Amen.

"*Oración del Campesino*" *por César Chávez (1927–93)*
Muéstrame el sufrimiento de los más desafortunados
para así conocer el dolor de mi pueblo.

Libérame para orar por los demás
pués tu estás presente en cada persona.

Ayúdame a tomar responsabilidad por mi propia vida
para que al fin pueda ser libre.

Concédeme la valentía para servir al prójimo
porque en la entrega hay vida verdadera.

Concédeme honradez y paciencia
para que podamos trabajar juntos.

Haz que el canto y la celebración
levanten el espíritu entre nosotros.

Haz que el espíritu florezca y crezca
para que no nos cansemos de la lucha.

Haznos recordar a los que han caído por la justicia,
porque ellos nos han dado la vida.

Ayúdanos a amar aún a los que nos odian
porque así podremos cambiar el mundo.

Amén.

– Session 3 –

Exploring the Meaning of Hope for the Writer of James and Ourselves

Goals for the Session

1. To obtain a deeper understanding of the notion of "hope."

2. To probe concepts of End Time and salvation.

3. To gain new insights into how our beliefs about hope and salvation affect how we live in the world.

Opening Worship

Scripture: James 5:7–11

Traditional Prayer in a Different Voice

Our Father, who art in heaven,
  Our Creator, you are all around us and within us.
Hallowed be Thy name
  We praise you with many different names.
Thy kingdom come, thy will be done
  Help us live as we understand we should from knowing you—
  In harmony and connectedness with each other.
On earth as it is in heaven.
  With all creatures of the earth, and with the earth and the universe itself.

Give us this day our daily bread.
**Help us to use your resources wisely so that we might
be sustained.**
And forgive our sins as we forgive those who sin
against us.
**Help us take responsibility when we fail to live
harmoniously, and help us
Understand and forgive when others let us down.**
And lead us not into temptation,
**Let us know you well enough that we are not tempted
to live outside of your love.**
But deliver us from evil.
And empower us to work together to overcome evil.
For thine is the kingdom and the power and the glory
forever.
**We believe that you created the world and that you
will be all around us and within us.**
Amen.
We are open to you.

C. Michael Hawn

– OR –

A Short Visual Meditation/Prayer

Show slides or a brief inspirational video. Contact your conference media office or library to borrow tapes of television
or radio spots for "Igniting Ministries." These are also available on-line for viewing and purchase at:
http://www.ignitingministry.org/spots/

Hymn

Select a hymn on the theme of hope such as:

"Hope of the World" (#178, *The United Methodist Hymnal*)

"My Hope Is Built" (#368, *The United Methodist Hymnal*)

"Be Thou My Vision" (#451, *The United Methodist Hymnal*)

"O God, Our Help in Ages Past" (#117, *The United Methodist Hymnal*)

"Song of Hope" "Canto de Esperanza" (#186, *The Faith We Sing*)

or "Tenemos Esperanza" "We Have Hope" (#59, *Global Praise 1*).

Primary Activities

1. Billboards/Ad Campaigns

Divide the class into small groups. Each group is to make a billboard using art supplies, magazine photos, etc. (which the facilitator will provide) to develop a PR/ad campaign for the End Time or for Salvation. Assign each group a specific perspective to use as the basis of the campaign. Possible perspectives are those of James; John Wesley; Martin Luther; religious movements today; secular figures such as Bill Gates; Oprah Winfrey; a NASA official or physicist like Stephen Hawking; an oil company CEO; an environmentalist; a well-known physician like Dr. Bernie Siegel (author of *Love, Medicine and Miracles*); a sports star like Derek Jeter; etc. Give each group 20 minutes to develop a slogan, the thrust of the PR/ad campaign, and make a "billboard" to present to the group. Then, in a large group, have each team present their billboard and campaign. Discuss each team's assumptions about

- who is saved
- what End Time is
- definitions
- desired actions on the part of people viewing the ad
- possible outcomes in this world of a particular interpretation of End Time and Salvation.

As each campaign is debriefed, consider:

- the connections between the promotion of a consumer society in the United States and a trend of more people claiming to be overtly religious

- the creation by a consumer culture of felt needs, wants, and insecurities

- how as a society or religious group we act out our personal and collective (social) salvation. Encourage participants to include racial/ethnic, gender, age, and class/economic status stereotypes and "messages" as major factors in this picture.

2. Video

Look in the current Service Center Catalog for the mission study theme AVs and other videos related to justice. Show the *Mission Magazine* video on the three current mission studies and possibly segments from one or more videos related to the mission studies on Mexico and Restorative Justice. Check your conference media center for videos on economic justice. Or show a segment from a commercially made video that has justice as a central theme, for example:

Erin Brockovitch	*Dead Man Walking*
The Hurricane	*A Lesson before Dying*
Romero	*The Milagro Beanfield War*
El Norte	*Long Walk Home*
City of Angels	*Places in the Heart*
The Mission	*Down and Out in Beverly Hills*
Harlan County	*Cry Freedom*

Discuss and identify where hope is evident in the video and how salvation is achieved for characters, if at all. Ask the group to imagine James's message to the major characters in the video. Assess the structural economic issues and other structural forms of oppression illustrated in the video. Pursue with the group how to address the root causes of the injustice. Where do they see signs of hope in their life or in the world today? Explore how one's economic position might affect how "hope" is identified and where hope is found. How do economics influence theology on a personal and community level?

3. *Bible Search*

Be sure to have several Bible translations available for the group's use and relevant materials from John Wesley's sermons. (See Appendix C, p. 154, for Web sites.) Ask small groups to scan James to locate use of the words "hope," "joy," and "happiness." Give each group a different edition of the Bible to use. Ask the participants to identify who is to be happy, joyous, or blessed.

- Why? How? What does this mean in the context of James?
- Are there important differences in the meanings of these words and how they are used in the various versions of the Bible?
- What does Elsa Tamez say about hope, happiness, and joy in James?
- How is Christian hope different from hope in a secular context?
- What does John Wesley have to say about hope, joy, and happiness?

4. *Guest Speakers or Site Visit*

Consider inviting one or more people to your session to share about difficult life experience and what hope and salvation mean to them. Possible guests might include:

- an immigrant
- a welfare recipient
- someone who has spent some time in jail or prison

- someone who has struggled to overcome an addiction

- an organizer for a community project dealing with economic inequalities in a more systemic and innovative way.

Alternatively, a site visit might be arranged to a local community project where participants can witness and possibly participate in justice-making work and talk with staff about what hope, salvation, and faith mean in their context.

5. Meditative Drawing

Invite participants to reflect individually on the reading related to the service of the poor and spiritual growth. Where are they now in the "spiritual map" provided by Father Nolan? (See Assignment #3, p. 128; also see Session 4, Activity 4, p. 141.) Can they think of examples of experiences they have had which fit one or more of the different approaches to service of the poor? Ask participants to sketch on their timeline their evolution in terms of their service with respect to people living in poverty. They may want to shade in different periods corresponding to the author's stages and note or draw symbols related to any special events that changed their attitude or behavior. What does Father Nolan have to say about how one views hope and salvation at each stage of the journey? Can participants see any connection between their own beliefs about hope and salvation and their approach to service? If there is time, have people share their journeys in a paired conversation with another participant.

Alternatively, the facilitator may choose to do some review and general discussion of the article in a large group and then break down into pairs or small groups for more extensive sharing or personal drawing or mapping time. (Note: a different suggestion for processing this material occurs in the suggestions for the last session under Activity 4, p. 141. Facilitators may want to do one or both activities.)

Suggested Assignments

1. Read chapters 4 and 5 in the study text.

2. Read James again (optional).

3. Research groups will need to finish preparing for the last class if this activity was assigned (see p. 111).

4. Add Step #3 on your personal timeline (see p. 152).

5. Do the silence exercise, if you haven't already (see p. 129).

Closing Hymn

Sing a hymn on the theme of hope, selecting another from the list for the opening meditation. Or sing one on the theme of rich and poor:

"We Meet You, O Christ" (#257, *United Methodist Hymnal*)

"Together We Serve" (#175, *The Faith We Sing*)

As the group is singing, consider having a vase with fresh flowers on the worship table and inviting everyone to take a flower and pin it on another participant as a symbol of hope. (Check in advance to make sure no one has allergies.)

Exploring How We Put Faith into Action—the Concept of Praxis

Goals for the Session

1. To probe what is meant by "militant patience."

2. To probe the challenges of personal integrity and honesty.

3. To evaluate the class—learnings, possible next steps on our own journeys. (It is left up to the facilitator to determine how to handle the evaluation. One possibility is to draw a spiral of praxis—experience, analysis, moral/religious reflection, action—and ask each person to comment about the class from these four points along the path. Regardless of how it is done, it is important for participants' closure and for the facilitator's own growth to allow sufficient time for the evaluation.)

Opening Worship

Scripture: James 1:3–4

Hymn

On the theme of justice. Possibilities include:

"For the Healing of the Nations" (#428, *The United Methodist Hymnal*)

"O Young and Fearless Prophet" (#444, *The United Methodist Hymnal*)

"The Voice of God Is Calling" (#436, *The United Methodist Hymnal*)

"All Who Love and Serve Your City" (#433, *The United Methodist Hymnal*)

"Where Cross the Crowded Ways of Life" (#427, *The United Methodist Hymnal*)

"What Does the Lord Require of You" (#174, *The Faith We Sing*)

"The Right Hand of God" (#60, *Global Praise 1*)

Primary Activities

1. Silence Experiment

If the silence experiment (p. 129) was assigned, ask for individual reports and group discussion of the results of this experiment. Use questions from the homework assignment as discussion starters. What did people learn about integrity, honesty, the power of speech, the power to withhold speech? Use this to lead into a discussion of the "perfect law of freedom"—a definition, and how we live it out today.

2. Research Group Reports

If this was assigned in Session 1 (see p. 111), allow plenty of time for reports and group discussion of them. Facilitators might want to ask the class or the research groups also to ponder whether they saw "militant patience" in any of the examples of faith in action.

- What are the challenges to individual and church integrity and honesty in each of these situations?
- What are the directives for focusing energies for change and organizing for effective action?

3. The Power of Prayer and Perseverance

As part of a group discussion about the meaning of "militant patience," ask a volunteer to read or act out Luke 18:1–8. Discuss what stance the widow took before the judge.

Can participants think of other historical examples where groups and individuals actively pursued justice for a long time, persevering against great odds?

- What are the lessons in these examples? Are there specific lessons about the power of prayer? The power of persistence? In how to organize and focus energies?

- Where do we need to take a strong collective stand today for economic justice? What might this feel like? Look like? What are the risks involved?

- What would we have to overcome individually to be part of this collective stance for economic justice?

- Writer and grassroots theologian Alice Walker asks us to live the future we dream about. What would be difficult for us in trying to align our lives more closely with our vision of economic justice?

(More honest and deeper sharing may occur on the last question if people break into pairs and take turns talking about their fears, feelings, ideas on how to move forward.)

4. Drama: The Service of the Poor and Stages of Spiritual Growth

Father Albert Nolan, O.P. (see #3 on p. 128) offers different stages of our faith journey with respect to economic justice.

Stage 1 is the development of compassion. In this phase we have experiences and gather information that provide exposure to the suffering of the poor. Through this exposure and through our willingness to cultivate our compassion, we are moved to action. Action in this phase tends to focus on charity and simplifying one's lifestyle.

Stage 2 involves discovering that poverty is a structural problem, not simply one of misfortune, laziness, bad luck, ignorance, or lack of development. Rather, it is the result of political and economic policies of governments and businesses. This can lead to indignation and anger. There are forms of righteous indignation and anger (see the Closing

Prayer, p. 144.) This can lead to trying to change systems and engaging in preventive political action.

Stage 3 begins with another discovery:

> that the poor must save themselves and that the poor will save themselves and that the poor don't really need you or me to save them.... Up to now we will have assumed that we must solve the problems of the poor either by bringing them relief or by changing the structures that oppress them... the realization that the poor know better than we do what needs to be done and how to do it may come as a surprise... they alone can do it.... Suddenly we are faced with the need to learn from the poor instead of teaching them.... They can and will save themselves with or without me, but I cannot be liberated without them.
>
> (http://www.bfpubs.demon.co.uk/service.htm)

A trap that could occur in Stage 3 would be romanticizing the poor and hero-worship.

Stage 4 "begins with the crisis of disillusionment and disappointment with the poor.... Poor and oppressed people do have faults, do commit sins, do make mistakes." "The poor are not saints and the rich sinners. Individuals cannot be praised for being poor or blamed for being rich, any more than they can be blamed for being poor and praised for being rich. There are exceptions... like those who become rich by exploiting the poor knowingly and intentionally." Stage 4 is a phase of solidarity where we take up the cause of the poor, not in a we-they fashion, but as in "us."

Use this framework to lead a discussion on people's own experiences, ascertaining where they are in their lived experience and emotions with respect to poverty. This can be a way to process what people learned in their personal timeline work. It is important to lead the discussion in a way that people can feel okay about being honest where they are in this process rather than competitive or fearful of judgment. One way to do this is to break into four small groups and assign each group to one of the stages. Each is to create a short skit illustrating a woman operating in that stage of understanding and awareness—to show the positive aspects of what she might do and the pitfalls for her and for the poor people with whom she is working.

5. *The Spiral of Praxis*

James and John Wesley, among others, call us to put our faith into action every moment of the day. This, in fact, is what "praxis" means. Draw a spiral on newsprint, or take masking tape and make one or more spirals on the floor of the room, marking points along the spiral's path. Use this graphic to lead a discussion about the reality of praxis. Ask participants to share how they saw the praxis spiral at work in their lives. (They can include sharing from their personal timelines if they did this assignment; see p. 112.)

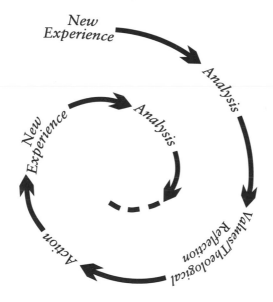

- Do they have a sense of the direction of their next phase of the journey?
- Where do they tend to get stuck in the spiral? Why?

- What can they do to get out of this "stuck" place?

- Where are the challenges to integrity and honesty in the spiral for them?

This could also be done as a kind of walking meditation—such as walking a maze or labyrinth. This spiral could also be used to facilitate the discussion on service with the poor and spiritual growth as a large or small group process or as a time of private, personal meditation.

Closing Worship

Prayer of Invocation

LEADER: To come before God in prayer is to surrender all the pride and all the walls that now divide us. Let us gather ourselves together then in prayer.

Almighty God, whose oneness gives the lie to all that separates your children, both our affluence and our wants are known to you, as is our slow desire to do your will. Let your Spirit quicken us to challenge the powers and the institutions that undermine the human spirit and to change the patterns of the world's existence that no one may countenance the continued separation of what you have joined together.

ALL: Through Christ our Lord. Amen.[b]

Hymn

Select a hymn on the theme of action, mercy, or justice. Some possibilities are:

---

b. This invocation is taken from "Banquet of Praise" from Bread for the World. Copyright © 1990 Bread for the World. Reprinted with permission of Bread for the World.

"God of Grace and God of Glory" (#577, *The United Methodist Hymnal*)

"Lord, Whose Love Through Humble Service" (#581, *The United Methodist Hymnal*)

"Lord, You Have Come to the Lake Shore" "Tú Has Venido a la Orilla" (#344, *The United Methodist Hymnal*)

"We Are One in Mission" (#243, *The Faith We Sing*)

"They'll Know We Are Christians by Our Love" (#223, *The Faith We Sing*)

"The Golden Rule She Has Pursued" (#53, *Global Praise 1*)

Personal Testimonies

Ask individuals to share a highlight of the study, a difficulty they see for themselves in moving forward, and a next step they are willing to take as an individual form of confession, praise, and commitment in a prayerful mode. Make sure everyone who wishes has a chance to speak.

Hymn

Select one:

#68, "Guide My Feet," *Global Praise 1;* or #593, "Here I Am, Lord," *The United Methodist Hymnal*

"Lord, You Have Come to the Lake Shore" "Tú Has Venido a la Orilla" (#344, *The United Methodist Hymnal*)

"The Spirit Sends Us Forth to Serve" (#241, *The Faith We Sing*)

"The Servant Song" (#222, *The Faith We Sing*)

"Sent Out In Jesus' Name" "Enviado Soy de Dios" (#184, *The Faith We Sing*)

"The Summons" (#130, *The Faith We Sing*)

Benediction

Holy One, help us not to remain indifferent and silent behind the safe security of stained-glass windows. We pray that we do not ignore the basic oppression that we participate in, ignoring what stares us in the face because life is much more comfortable and convenient that way. Give us the courage to stand amid social evil and serve as a headlight, not a taillight—a powerful voice, not a weak echo. Help us to substitute courage for caution, clarity for confusion. Deepen our faith so that we may work passionately, unrelentingly to bring good out of evil. Give us the power that we need. We often see examples of how power without love is reckless and abusive. Help us to understand that, equally, love without power is sentimental and anemic. Power at its best is love implementing the demands of justice. Justice at its best is power correcting everything that stands against love. Dear God, guide our feet once again to demand justice and to stand for love. Amen.[c]

---

c. Adapted from a eulogy given by the Rev. Dr. Martin Luther King, Jr. for the Rev. James Reeb, who was killed by white supremacists in Selma, Alabama, in 1965; and from Dr. King's last speech to the SCLC in 1967. The entire text of the eulogy was published in the May/June 2001 issue of *UU World*, pp. 20–23. The sentences about love and power are from a 1967 speech included in *A Testament of Hope* (New York: HarperCollins, 1991).

– *Appendix A* –

Sample Exegetical Exercises

Listed below are some exercises designed to help participants interpret Scripture (the meaning of "exegetical") and address some of the controversy surrounding the authorship of James and its messages. Pick and choose among them according to their relevance to the lesson plan you develop and the interests and capacities of participants. Facilitators may want to do some of these exercises in advance for their own preparation or to practice presenting them to the class.

1. Photocopy the Letter of James. Ask participants to highlight in one color all the statements that sound Jewish in background and then to highlight the particularly Christian statements in a second color. Finally they are to look for elements that might be Greco-Roman in character and use a third color to highlight these. Does this tell you anything about who James was? Who his audience was?

2. Frances Taylor Gench notes that "some commentators claim that the Sermon on the Mount in its entirety is paralleled in James."[d] Photocopy James and Matthew 5–7 and Luke 6:17–49, the Sermon on the Mount. Examine the three texts to see which version of the Sermon on the Mount seems more similar to James. Cut up James and the versions of the Sermon and paste them side by side. You might have James copied on a different color paper so you can see each text

---

d. Frances Taylor Gench, "Hebrews and James," *Westminster Bible Companion* (Louisville: Westminster John Knox Press, 1998), 83.

more clearly once it is pasted up. Does the parallel work? Do you think the writer of James was familiar with the Sermon?

3. Luther criticized the Letter of James for not focusing enough on Jesus Christ. Go through the text of James and circle every reference to Jesus. Then go through it and circle every reference to God.

- Is there any reference to the Holy Spirit?
- Is it enough to speak about God?
- Is Christ implicit when James says God?
- What does it mean for the Trinity to be three in one?
- In your own life, do you speak more often of Jesus, God, or the Holy Spirit?
- Does this affect your ethical approach to life? Your spiritual approach to life?

4. The "faith without works is dead" statement sounds like it contradicts Paul. Use your concordance or the Web site **www.biblegateway.com** to search on words like "liberty," "faith," "law," and "world." Is there a similarity to Paul's use of "fruits of the spirit" and James's "works"? You might again photocopy sections and paste them side by side to compare them. You could also compare Paul's exhortations to the Corinthians to James's exhortations.

5. Another interesting comparison is between James 2:17–26 and Hebrews 11 on the nature of faith. (Most scholars do not think Paul wrote Hebrews since he usually spoke of himself and his experiences in his other letters.) You could continue the comparison between Hebrews 12 on suffering and the nature of service and leadership in Hebrews 13 with the James texts about suffering in 1:12–18 and 5:7–11.

6. Examine the use of the word "judgment" in terms of ethical exhortation, works, faith, hope, and the end times.

Start with James 2:12–14, go to Luke 10:13–15, and then Matthew 10:14–16, 11:21–25, and 12:35–37. Expand your search from there. John uses the word "judgment" extensively but with a unique character.

7. After studying the content of James closely, what would you say was going on inside the church and outside the church at that time?

- Are the rich people whom James addresses outside the church or inside the church?

- What does it mean if they are outside? Inside?

- What reversals of behavior characterize his commands to the rich and to the poor? Reflect on the reversals in the Beatitudes ("Blessed are they who . . . ").

- Look at the other issues raised; were they inside or outside the church?

- Would we fit inside the church or outside the church in James's estimation?

8. Do you think James was a real letter, or are there elements that normally go in letters that are missing? Compare James to other short letters in the epistles to examine the common elements of a letter in that day.

9. Would you consider this writing to be similar to Wisdom literature such as Proverbs and Jesus' use of parables and the Beatitudes, or more like that of the Prophets? In what ways does it resonate with each genre or type of literature? In what ways do these writings overlap?

– *Appendix B* –

Questions for
a Personal Timeline

Step #1: Your Economic History

a. What were the immediate economic circumstances you were born into? Draw a small symbol of this on your timeline where it starts, next to your birth date.

b. What kind of economic circumstances were your society and country experiencing when you were born (examples: a war, a depression, an economic crisis, a boom time)? Draw a symbol of this on your timeline, showing how long the period lasted.

c. How did these economic circumstances—both personal and in the larger world—influence your assumptions about the world and your position in it as you were growing up? Do you still hold any of these assumptions?

d. Did you experience any major changes in economic circumstances as a child, youth, or adult? If so, when? Why? Mark these points on your timeline with a symbol or picture and date (examples: marriage, divorce, health crisis, disability, receiving an inheritance). How did the change affect your view about what you thought was "normal" or what you took for granted?

e. As you were growing up, what was your attitude about money? About work? About charity and giving? Has this changed at all? When? How?

f. Think of key moments in your life when you received money for work done (examples: after-school job, baby-sitting, your first paid job, major employment changes, a period of unemployment, retirement). Put some dates and symbols on your timeline to chart these events.

   g. Mark on the timeline key moments related to important unpaid work (examples: major volunteer efforts, becoming a stay-at-home parent, working in a food pantry or thrift shop, being the primary caregiver for parents, grandchildren). Again, use symbols and dates showing the time period for which this activity was important in your life.

   h. Mark on the timeline when you first came to grips with what it meant to be "poor" (related to either your own or someone else's situation). What happened? What did you realize? Were there other events related to your understanding of poverty? Mark these on your chart with symbols and approximate dates if you can remember them.

   i. When did you first realize there were enormous differences in incomes and wealth among people in your town or city, state, and country? What happened? How did you feel? Add a symbol or picture and rough date to record this. Are there other important learnings and experiences to put on your chart related to economic inequality?

   j. Mark on the timeline when you first realized there were enormous differences in people's circumstances in different countries. What happened? How did you feel? Are there other major events and learnings related to global inequalities to put on your chart?

   k. If there are other key moments in your life that altered your economic status or views, add them to your timeline.

Step #2: Your Faith Journey

   a. At the time of your birth, what were the spiritual or religious beliefs of your primary caregivers? Make a symbol of this to put next to your birth and shade or otherwise mark the time period for which this held.

   b. Mark on your timeline the date of your baptism. If you were confirmed into church membership, mark this date.

c. If you have gone through important evolutions in your religious identity, mark these moments or periods on your timeline (examples: converted from one faith to another, joined The United Methodist Church, changed denominational membership), with dates and a symbol or picture.

d. Try to remember the first experience you had of the Holy, of something sacred, of a mystery larger than you, of experiencing grace. Mark this on your timeline. Add any subsequent similar moments.

e. Have you experienced any time when you lost hope or your belief in God was tested? If so, add this to your timeline. When did it happen? What happened? How was the faith crisis resolved?

f. Think about how your understanding of God has evolved. Can you identify certain pivotal moments or characterize your beliefs into certain time periods? Try to mark this on your timeline.

g. Mark the periods of membership in different churches or congregations with dates and symbols or a small note. What was the social and economic profile of each? Is there a correlation between the kind of church you joined and your socioeconomic status? How has your church membership shaped your reading of the Bible? Your understanding of poverty? The choices you have made in your life?

Step #3: Your History of Social Concern and Action

a. When did you first sense life was not always fair to you? To others? How did this happen? How did you respond? Mark this on your timeline with a date if possible and symbols.

b. Have there been other occasions in your life where you experienced or witnessed great injustice? How did you respond? Mark these on your timeline. Have these experiences changed your views at all?

c. How did you come to learn what charity was? Has your understanding of charity changed over time? Mark any highlights on your timeline with dates, symbols, or pictures. This will complement any work you did on your timeline using the Nolan article, if the facilitator assigned this task (see #3 on p. 128).

    d. What are some major acts of charity in which you have engaged? What do you feel you accomplished? Mark these as events or periods in your life on your timeline.

    e. Have you tried to work on the root causes of economic or another form of injustice? How? When? What did you learn? What did you accomplish? Add this to your timeline with dates and symbols.

Now look over all three layers or pieces of your timeline— your economic history, your faith journey, and the history of social concern and action. Do any interesting connections pop out? Do you see any patterns developing? Do you see any of the three "layers" (economic, spiritual, action) influencing another? Are there any surprises? What insights about your life have you gained as a result of this exercise?

– *Appendix C* –

Resources

Where to Go for More Information

For More Theological Help

Related Sermons of John Wesley. (All are in public domain and can be printed and copied for use in a classroom setting.)

On Christian Perfection
   http://gbgm-umc.org/umhistory/wesley/sermons/serm-040.stm
   http://gbgm-umc.org/umhistory/wesley/sermons/serm-076.stm

The Cure of Evil Speaking
   http://gbgm-umc.org/umhistory/wesley/sermons/serm-049.stm

The Good Steward
   http://gbgm-umc.org/umhistory/wesley/sermons/serm-051.stm

On Riches
   http://gbgm-umc.org/umhistory/wesley/sermons/serm-087.stm
   http://gbgm-umc.org/umhistory/wesley/sermons/serm-108.stm
   http://gbgm-umc.org/umhistory/wesley/sermons/serm-126.stm

The Use of Money
   http://gbgm-umc.org/umhistory/wesley/sermons/serm-050.stm

On Dress
   http://gbgm-umc.org/umhistory/wesley/sermons/serm-088.stm

On Patience
   http://gbgm-umc.org/umhistory/wesley/sermons/serm-083.stm

The Women's Division spiritual growth studies on James and John Wesley, see:
    http: //gbgm-umc.org/umw/james and
    http: //gbgm-umc.org/umw/wesley respectively.

On Wesley and Scripture, including Wesley's translation and Notes on James:
    http: //wesley.nnu.edu/wesley_NT

Text comparisons paragraph by paragraph from many different versions of the Bible can be found at:
    http: //www.innvista.com/scriptures/compare/epistle.htm

To browse the World Wide Study Bible on the Christian Classics Ethereal Library page:
    http: //ccel.org/wwsb

The Biblical Studies Foundation includes links to many other sites:
    http: //www.bible.org

The Virtual Religion Index of the Religion Department at Rutgers University includes biblical studies, Christian traditions, and others:
    http: //www.religion.rutgers.edu/vri

For a useful course on liberation theology from the Henry George Institute, plus good links to other sites:
    http: //www.landreform.org

Faith-Based Justice Web Sites

General Board of Global Ministries
    http: //www.gbgm-umc.org

General Board of Church and Society
    http: //www.umc-gbcs.org

Faith and Social Justice page:
    http: //www.geocities.com/capitolhill/1764

Evangelicals for Social Action:
    http: //www.esa-online.org/esa.html

Islam and Social Justice page:
http://www.wco.com/~altaf/altaf.html

Shoestrings and Grace: the Strategic Pastoral Action
Network (SPAN):
http://www.lightlink.com/wrehberg

Sojourners magazine and community online:
http://www.sojo.net

Organizations Addressing Themes
Related to the James Study

Living Wage Campaigns

Jobs with Justice
501 Third Street, NW
Washington, DC 20001
Phone: 202-434-1106; Fax: 202-434-1477
Web site: http://www.jwj.org
*Click on "organizing tools" for a Religious Action kit, information
about welfare reform, and information on wage conditions around
the country.*

National Inter-Faith Committee for Worker Justice
1020 West Bryn Mawr Avenue, 4th floor
Chicago, IL 60660
Phone: 773-728-8400; Fax: 773-728-8409
Web site: http://www.nicwj.org
*Produces faith-based resources on a range of subjects. Click
on "issues" for their tools and information about living wage
campaigns.*

ACORN
739 Eighth Street, SE
Washington, DC 20003
Phone: 202-547-2500; Fax 202-546-2483
Web site: http://www.livingwagecampaign.org
*A comprehensive site listing all the living wage cities, sample
ordinances, summaries of winning campaigns, etc.*

Welfare Reauthorization and Antipoverty Campaigns

Applied Research Center
Rev. Susan Starr
3781 Broadway
Oakland, CA 94611
Phone: 510-653-3415; Fax: 510-653-3427
Web site: **http://www.arc.org**
Check the Welfare Advocacy Research Project and links with other related groups. Staff member Rev. Starr resources a national coalition of fifty groups working on welfare reauthorization.

Center for Budget and Policy Priorities
820 First Street, NE
Washington, DC 20002
Phone: 202-408-1080; Fax 202-408-1056
Web site: **http://www.cbpp.org**
A good nongovernmental source for U.S. poverty data. Specializes in producing easy-to-read, thoughtful, credible analyses of current welfare programs and their impact. Summaries of the latest national poverty and income trends available on the Web site.

Center for Community Change
1000 Wisconsin Avenue, NW, #B
Washington, DC 20007
Phone: 202-342-0567; Fax: 202-333-5462
Web site: **http://www.communitychange.org**
Also has an office in San Francisco. Staff provides support to a major national coalition working on welfare reauthorization.

Institute for Women's Policy Research
1707 L Street, NW, Suite 750
Washington, DC 20036
Phone: 202-785-5100; Web site: **http://www.iwpr.org**
The leading national think tank monitoring women's economic status and policy initiatives in the United States with a focus on welfare policy, employment issues, etc. Includes statistics and issue briefs, among other items.

Kensington Welfare Rights Union
P.O. Box 50678
Philadelphia, PA 19134
Phone: 215-203-1945; Fax: 215-203-1950
Web site: **http://www.kwru.org**
An example of what one welfare rights organization is doing. This Web site's links include the "University of the Poor" (**www.universityofthepoor.org**). *Promotes information sharing and organizing among poor people. Also includes a section for people of faith for acting in solidarity; click on: "School of Theology."*

The Linc Project
Welfare Law Center
275 Seventh Avenue, Suite 1205
New York, NY 10001
Phone: 212-633-6967; Web site: **http://www.lincproject.org**
An excellent, comprehensive site listing many grassroots groups working on welfare reauthorization and poverty in the United States.

Network: The Catholic Social Justice Lobby
801 Pennsylvania Avenue, SE, Suite 460
Washington, DC 20003-2167
Phone: 202-547-5556; Fax: 202-547-5510
Web site: **http://www.networklobby.org**
Hotline (for legislative updates): 202-547-5573
Has selected welfare reauthorization and poverty as a top priority. Offers training materials and workshops open to all to assist faith-based organizing across the United States (in English and Spanish). Also monitors at the state level the impact of welfare reform on women. Welcomes collaboration with people of faith.

Farmworkers Movement

Farm Labor Organizing Committee
1221 Broadway Street
Toledo, OH 43609
Phone: 419-243-3456; Fax: 419-243-5655
e-mail only: **floc@accesstoledo.com**

United Farmworkers of America
P.O. Box 62
Keene, CA 93531
Phone: 661-823-6252; Fax 661-823-6177
Web site: http://www.ufw.org
Lists regional offices and current campaigns, and provides solidarity ideas. Also has links to related groups and efforts.

National Farm Worker Ministry
438 N. Skinker Blvd.
St. Louis, MO 63130
Phone: 314-726-6470; Fax: 314-726-6427
Web site: http://www.nfwm.org
This Web site offers a range of helpful information, including links to national and regional farmworker groups.

Zapatista Movement

Several Web sites offer extensive information. A good place to begin is http://www.zapatistas.org, *the official site that provides links to many others. For information in English on Bishop Samuel Ruiz and his successor (very active in peace negotiations between the Zapatistas and the Mexican government), see* http://www.peacecouncil.org. *This site for the interfaith global peace effort tracks what is happening in Chiapas among other hot spots. If you read Spanish, two excellent Web sites are those from the Diocese of San Cristóbal de las Casas (covers Chiapas) at* http://www.laneta.apc.org/curiasc *and the Fray Bartolomé de las Casas independent human rights office in Chiapas at* http://www.laneta.apc.org/cdhbcasas. *See* http://www.Amazon.com *for a listing of books and videos on the movement.*

Jubilee Movement

Jubilee 2000 USA
222 East Capitol Street, NW
Washington, DC 20003
Phone: 202-783-3566; Fax: 202-546-4468
Web site: http://www.j2000usa.org
The primary Web site for the global Jubilee movement is http://www.jubilee2000uk.org, *which lists all country contacts*

*and current actions. Note: Many Jubilee Web sites have nothing
to do with this movement. Carefully type in the correct address.
Jubilee 2000 USA has local groups around the country.*

Free Trade/Fair Trade

Fifty Years: Network for Global Economic Justice
3628 Twelfth Street, NE
Washington, DC 20017
Phone: 202-IMF-BANK; Web site: **igc.org**
*Publishes newsletter and conducts educational events on the latest
developments related to debt cancellation, structural adjustment
policies, reforming the International Monetary Fund and the
World Bank, and related issues. Also has affiliated local groups
around the country.*

Inter-faith Working Group on International Trade & Investment
c/o Maria Riley
Center of Concern
1225 Otis Street, NE
Washington, DC 20017
Phone: 202-635-2757; e-mail: **iwg@coc.org**
*Produced an interfaith statement of principles designed to promote
dialogue on the content of just and sustainable trade and investment policies. Religious institutions are invited to endorse the
statement. Many Protestant, Catholic, Jewish and other religious
groups have already endorsed it. Contact the e-mail address for
more information.*

American Friends Service Committee
Democratizing the Global Economy Project
1501 Cherry Street
Philadelphia, PA 19102
Phone: 215-241-7000; Fax: 215-241-7119
Web site: **http://www.afsc.org**
*The project operates in several cities, focusing on trade agreements
and the Free Trade Agreement of the Americas in particular.
AFSC's Web site offers much information on trade and other
economic issues of interest for this study. Click on "Issues" to
get an extensive list of programs, goals, and locations of projects.
Click on "free trade" for information on DGE.*

Public Citizen
Global Trade Watch Program
215 Pennsylvania Avenue, SE
Washington, DC 20003
Phone: 202-546-4996; Fax: 202-547-7392
Web site: http://www.citizen.org
Has organizers and field offices across the country, and is a key
place to check for current campaigns, legislative updates, etc. from
a secular point of view.

World Trade Organization
Geneva, Switzerland
Web site: http://www.wto.org
See the home page for access to nongovernmental organization
(NGO) briefings, events, trade statistics, and annual WTO reports.

SERRV/10,000 Villages
These two faith-based projects were pioneers in the "fair trade"
movement. They sell a variety of handicrafts from producer co-ops
around the world. One of the prime commodities offered currently
through fair trade is coffee, from distributors such as Thanksgiving
Coffee, Equal Exchange, and others. The Women's Division has a
policy encouraging the use of fair trade coffee and tea throughout
the organization of UMW. Contact UMOUN, 777 UN Plaza,
New York, NY 10017, for more details or go to the web site at:
http://secure.serrv.org/SERRVtest/SERRV/catalog.

The Women's Division's Office of Economic Justice and United
Methodist Women *have a long history of involvement in the*
suggested issues above. For more information about church and
Division policies and current activities related to these issues,
contact:
Executive Secretary for Economic Justice, Women's Division
475 Riverside Drive, Room 1500
New York, NY 10115
Phone: 212-870-3766; e-mail: **mclement@gbgm-umc.org**

Glossary

Alpheus: the father of one of the disciples of Jesus.

anachronistic: from the wrong time period. Anachronisms in writing usually indicate the writing was done later than the event depicted.

androcentric (from **androcentrism**): term from the Greek that signifies the centrality of the male (*andr-*), or that everything revolves around men.

antithetical: opposite.

apocalypse, apocalyptic: the final cataclysmic revelation of God's plan for the world, punishing the wicked and persecutors of the truth while vindicating the faithful who endured fierce trials and persecution.

apostolic authority/authorship: the tradition that most New Testament documents were written by Christ's apostles and therefore share the special grace and authority of Christ himself.

beatitude: literally, state of blessing; specifically the verses in Matthew and Luke that begin "blessed are."

biblical criticism: the application of literary, historical, and other critical methods to study of the Bible.

canon: from the Latin and Greek word for "rule": a list or body of documents agreed upon as authoritative. The authority of a canon comes from the people who agree to accept it, but the canon may later be given authority in itself, especially if it is regarded as closed or finalized. A canon can be seen as a fixed revelation or as a work in progress, depending on which view holds more authority among its adherents. Today's churches consider the biblical canon closed, so that nothing can be added as "Scripture," but at the time of Jesus or Paul it was not.

Christology: the study of the person and work of Christ, the "anointed one," or Messiah, of the Christian faith. The church's understanding of the nature of Christ has developed over centuries and was a major focus of the early councils that systematized the religion.

Clement of Rome: bishop of the Christian community in Rome just after the apostolic period (about 96 c.e.), and author of several letters that were almost accepted as Scripture.

concupiscence: selfish desire, the human tendency toward sin.

cosmological theology: explanation of how the world (*kosmos*) came to be and God's relation to it.

Deuteronomist: the final editor of the books of Deuteronomy, Joshua, Judges, Samuel, and Kings.

diaspora: the Greek word for the Jewish communities living dispersed outside Jerusalem in ancient times, mostly in large cities such as Alexandria, Corinth, and Rome. Some of these communities had forty or fifty thousand Jews who formed significant portions of their populations.

diatribe: an intermediate form between a treatise and a dialogue. The author invents an adversary with whom he maintains a dialogue, using questions that are sometimes ironic.

Dispersion: English for *diaspora* (see above).

ephemeral: vanishing, short-lasting; literally "a day long."

Erasmus, Desiderius (c. 1466–1536): Renaissance philosopher and theologian who published a Greek text of the New Testament as part of an effort to return Christian study to its sources. Erasmus influenced many Reformers but never left the Catholic Church himself.

eschatology, eschatological: the study of the end (Greek *eschaton*) of the world and the "last things" pertaining to it. New Testament last things include the last judgment and second coming of Christ. Different Christian views interpret the End as literal, symbolic, futuristic, or realized, or a number of other things.

exegesis, exegete: Greek for "interpretation" or interpreter; the explanation of the meaning of Scripture texts, or the person interpreting them.

form criticism: the study of biblical texts by looking at the literary genres that form their backgrounds and contexts and usually relate to the historical circumstances as well.

hapax legomenon (pl. *hapax legomena*): name given to a word that appears only once in the biblical text.

Hebrew Bible: the biblical books written in Hebrew, largely the same as what Christians call the Old Testament or Jewish Bible. This includes the Torah (or Pentateuch), the Prophets, and the Writings. (The Apocrypha were Jewish books written in Greek.)

Hellenic: Greek, or influenced by the Greek culture spread throughout the Eastern Mediterranean lands, including Palestine, by Alexander the Great around 300 B.C.E.

Hermas: An early second-century Christian teacher in the area around Rome. His most famous writing is *The Shepherd*. Almost included in the Bible, it was omitted because Hermas was not a first-generation apostle.

interpolation: the addition of text by an editor or copyist to interpret or embellish the received text.

logocentric societies: societies that hold there is an ultimate truth or meaning in texts that forms the basis of all other meaning. Western, Eurocentric, or American societies are essentially logocentric.

Luther, Martin (1483–1546): German monk who broke with the Church of Rome over papal authority and the sale of indulgences, effectively starting the Protestant Reformation. He posted the ninety-five theses of his protest to the cathedral door in Wittenberg in 1517. His followers became known as Lutherans.

Maccabees: leaders of a triumphant revolt of oppressed Jews against the tyrannous rule of the Syrian Greek king Antiochus IV in 168 B.C.E. The festival of Hanukkah marked their rededication of the Temple in Jerusalem. Some Bibles include two, three, or four Books of the Maccabees describing these events. Protestant Bibles place them among the Apocrypha.

makarios: Greek word translated as "happy" and "blessed"; the word beginning all the Beatitudes, and also (in its feminine form) describing Mary in Luke 1:45.

makrothymia: Greek word meaning literally "large spirit"; translated as "patience."

marginalize(d), marginalization: completely or mostly left out of the predominant economic and cultural power structure in a society.

pagan: from the Latin word for "country dweller," someone living outside the city and its culture. In the New Testament, Jews referred to non-Jews as Gentiles or pagans.

paradox: something that is true although its opposite is also true (such as Christ died, yet lives).

paraenesis, paraenetic: Greek word for exhortation or moral instruction.

parousia: Greek word for "coming" or "advent," used in reference to Christ's return or Second Coming.

patriarchal: from patriarchy, a system of social, economic, political, and legal relationships in which the father is the head of the family and the entire household depends on him. In this system the condition of women is usually one of submission. Most well-known ancient societies were strongly patriarchal.

perfect, perfection: English translation of the Greek words (*teleios, telos, teleio*), which mean more accurately "completed, fulfilled, matured" rather than the English sense of "without flaw." John Wesley stressed Christian perfection.

polemic: a strong argument; from the Greek word for "war."

praxis: practice; the living out of religious or philosophical beliefs. It is used in liberation theologies to mean action combined with reflection seeking to transform oppressive situations or social orders.

pseudonym: literally, a false name. It was commonplace in the ancient world for writers to enhance the authority of their writing by attributing it to a better known or respected figure, like the Apostle Paul. Many writings not accepted into the biblical canon were also attributed to better known figures, such as the Gospel of Philip or the Apocalypse of Moses. The presence of anachronisms is one clue that a document might have been attributed to someone other than the actual writer.

rabbinic tradition: the form of Judaism that developed after the destruction of the Temple in 70 C.E., consisting of discussions among schools of rabbis and disciples to interpret Scripture. The interpretations were written down as the Mishnah and the Talmud over the next few centuries.

redaction, redactional: the editing and ordering of written materials by someone other than the writer. Redaction criticism studies such editing work and draws conclusions from what has been moved or left out or condensed, and what the editors' purposes might have been.

reductionism: oversimplification; trying to fit complex ideas into an interpretation that denies or omits their complexity. **Theological reductionism** is the effort to explain complex theological ideas in terms that are not sufficient to describe them, or to fit them into a theory of, e.g., philosophy or psychology.

Semitic, Semite: language or ethnic designation traditionally attributed to the descendants of Shem, son of Noah. Colloquially it usually refers to Jews; however Arabs are also Semitic. Arabic as well as Hebrew are Semitic languages.

Septuagint: from the Latin for "seventy"; often abbreviated LXX. The Greek translation of the Jewish Scriptures, completed about a century before Christ. According to tradition, seventy (or seventy-two) rabbis worked on it. The Septuagint was the early church's Scriptures. It included the Apocrypha.

Sitz im Leben: German phrase meaning "setting in life"; the specific context in which a biblical text was written, relating that text to the history and circumstances of the writer's life.

solifidianism: a term used to caricature or mock the Reformation doctrine of justification "by faith alone," Latin *sola fide.*

transparency: accountability based on clarity and openness.

variant: an alternative text of great age and authenticity, acknowledged by scholars but not necessarily by tradition. Scriptural variants sometimes lead to controversy.

Additional Resources

Printed Resources Available from The United Methodist Church and the General Board of Global Ministries Service Center

The Book of Resolutions of the United Methodist Church, 2000. Available from Cokesbury, 1-800-672-1789, $14.00.

The Faith We Sing. Supplement to *The United Methodist Hymnal.* Available from Cokesbury; see above. $10.00.

Kimbrough, ST, Jr. *Resistless Love: Christian Witness in the New Millennium (A Wesleyan Perspective).* #2846, $7.95.

————.*Who Are the People Called Methodists?* Booklet. #2901, $1.50.

More Stories Along the Way. Church and community workers since 1885. #2897, $8.00.

New World Outlook. The mission magazine of The United Methodist Church, $15.00 a year (six issues); $26.00 for two years. See *Response* for combination subscription information.

Prayer Calendar 2003. #3179, $7.50.

Putting Children and Their Families First. Handbook to help congregations assess needs and develop ministries with families. #2627, $4.75; five or more, $4.27 each.

Response. The magazine for United Methodist Women. Subscriptions, $12.00 a year (11 issues); $22.00 for two years. In combination with *New World Outlook*, $25.00 a year; $45.00 special two-year rate. A thirtieth-anniversary CD-ROM is also available. #2821, $30.00.

Telling Our Stories. Booklet of a hundred stories detailing mission institutions and people whose lives have changed because of them. #2842, $5.00.

World Trade Organization: In Whose Hands? Packet of materials to facilitate understanding of the WTO and its economic impact around the world. #2939, $5.00.

Young Adult Mission Service Opportunities. Booklet of descriptions and instructions for mission programs available through the General Board of Global Ministries. Available from the Office of Youth and Young Adults, Room 320, 475 Riverside Drive, New York, NY 10115.

Yrigoyen, Charles, Jr. *John Wesley: Holiness of Heart and Life.* Study Guide by Ruth Daugherty. Eng. #2543, Span. #2544, Kor. #2545, $4.50.

Brochures

Mission Volunteers. Describes opportunities for interested individuals and groups. #5375, free for postage and handling.

Opportunities for Individual Volunteers. Information and instructions for individuals or couples to volunteer for two months or more. #5497, free for postage and handling.

To Call: To Send—Mission Volunteers. Six-page leaflet highlights mission opportunities for individuals and groups, and contact information to follow up. #5487, free for postage and handling.

United Methodist NOMADS in the 21st Century. Mission opportunities for people with recreational vehicles and time. #5528, free for postage and handling.

Youth & Young Adults Changing Our World. Four pages describe programs, opportunities, offices, and resources available for young people through the General Board of Global Ministries. #5511, free for postage and handling.

Poster

Global Justice Volunteers Poster. 11" x 17" poster about an overseas program for eighteen- to twenty-four-year-olds. #5479, free for postage and handling.

Music

Faith · Hope · Love: Songs for the New Millennium. Contemporary Christian songs from around the world. CD #2922, $12.95; Cassette #2924, $8.95.

Global Praise 1. Collection of international Christian songs. CD #2565, $12.95; Cassette #2566, $8.95.

Global Praise 1. Songbook. 96 pages; #2572, $6.95.

Global Praise 2. Sixteen songs in eight languages. CD #2921, $12.95; Cassette #2920, $8.95.

Global Praise 2: Songs for Worship and Witness. 127 songs; #2918, $8.95.

Kimbrough, ST, Jr. *Songs for the Poor: Hymns of Charles Wesley.* Singers' edition of thirteen hymns. #1846, $3.00.

On-Line Resources

Here are some selected Internet addresses relating to biblical and theological studies, poverty and wealth and social justice issues. (Note: Many Web sites are frequently updated. Sometimes the site names or other details change. The information offered here is accurate as of January 2002. The Women's Division will keep an up-to-date list of links on its Web site at: **http: //gbgm-umc.org/ umw/james.** If you encounter problems, use the e-mail address there to communicate with staff.) See also Appendix C on p. 154.

United Methodist and Women's Division On-Line Resources

For the Women's Division spiritual growth study on James, see the GBGM site:
http: //gbgm-umc.org/umw/james

Women's Division Web pages on past spiritual growth studies of related interest:
2002 Jesus and Courageous Women:
http: //gbgm-umc.org/umw/jesusandwomen
1997 John Wesley:
http: //gbgm-umc.org/umw/wesley

General Board of Global Ministries. Web site:
http: //gbgm-umc.org.

United Methodist Board of Church and Society. Web site:
http: //www.umc-gbcs.org.

Religious Task Force on Central America and Mexico:
http: //www.rtfcam.org

Mark Goodacre's excellent, comprehensive New Testament Gateway site:

   http: //www.ntgateway.com

The excellent site *Diotima: Materials for Study on Women and Gender in the Ancient World* has a good section on biblical studies:

   http: //www.stoa.org/diotoma

Hanson and Oakman's *Palestine in the Time of Jesus: Social Structures and Social Conflicts:*

   http: //www.stolaf.edu/people/kchanson/ptj.html

Index of Scriptural References

Index of Authors

A Women's Division publication produced by the
General Board of Global Ministries
The United Methodist Church

Please mail order with check payable to:
SERVICE CENTER
P.O. BOX 691328
CINCINNATI OH 45269-1328

COSTS FOR SHIPPING AND HANDLING:

Sale items:	Free items:
$25 or less, add $4.65	50 copies or less, $3.50
$25.01–$60, add $5.75	51–400, $4.50
$60.01–$100, add $7.00	Over 400, $1.50 per 100
Over $100, add 6.5%	

Revised formula effective March 15, 2002

For billed or credit card orders
CALL TOLL FREE: 1-800-305-9857
If billing is requested, a $1.50 billing fee will be added.
FAX ORDERS: 1-513-761-3722

**SERVICE CENTER
7820 READING ROAD CALLER NO 1800
CINCINNATI OH 45222-1800**

chlorine-free paper

$6.00   AC/LE 3/02   Stock #3193